The Ultimate

Swedish Cookbook

111 Dishes From Sweden To Cook Right Now

Slavka Bodic

Imprint: Independently published

Please sign up for free Balkan and Mediterranean recipes:
www.balkanfood.org

Introduction

One of the largest Scandinavian countries- Sweden, has a large expanse, extending from north to south in Northern Europe. The country, therefore, has vast diversity in its traditional cuisine. The region is known for its distinct culture and languages, which is also influenced by other major European countries like France, Germany, etc.

The great benefit about Swedish food is that it isn't only tasty, but it's also rich in healthy and nutritious ingredients. It offers your number of unique combinations of fruits, vegetables, grains, beans, legumes, seafood, and meat, etc. Some if you're curious about Swedish cuisine and want to explore all its different flavors, then this cookbook delivers the perfect match for you!

The Ultimate Swedish Cookbook will introduce you to Swedish cuisine and its culinary culture in a way that you must have never tried before. It brings you a variety of Swedish recipes in one place. The book is great for all those who are always keen to cook healthy food and want to explore its unique flavors. With the help of this Swedish cuisine cookbook, you can create a complete Swedish menu at home, or you can try all the special Swedish recipes on your own with minimum effort and less kitchen time. In this cookbook, you'll further find popular Swedish meals and the ones that you might not have heard of yet. From nourishing Swedish bread to all of the strong drinks, exotic desserts, main dishes, and Swedish salads, etc., you can find them all. And all these recipes are created in such a simple way that those who aren't even familiar with the Swedish culture, food, and language can still try and cook them at home, without facing much difficulty.

In sum, Swedish culinary culture and cuisine are full of surprises. You'd never expect to have a mix of all the European cuisines all in one place, but Swedish food makes that possible with its Scandinavian, Germanic, and European Influences. And if you want to bring all those flavors to your dinner table, then give this book a thorough read, and you'll uncover all the answers in one place.

Let's try all these Swedish Recipes and recreate a complete menu to celebrate the amazing Swedish flavors and unforgettable aromas!

Table Of Contents

Why Swedish Cuisine?

Swedish cuisine is diverse because of the influences of both its northern and southern regions. People from the north, due to their climatic conditions, enjoy more of the reindeer or other meats, stews, fats like cheese and lards, etc. Whereas the people in the southern regions prefer fruit, veggies, grains, and legumes in their diets more often. Despite the regional differences, there are few commonly used ingredients which are the characteristic features of Swedish cuisine like:

- Lingonberries
- Rye
- Reindeer meat
- Pork
- Lamb

Traditionally Swedes have been open to foreign culinary influences, ranging from French cuisine to Chinese sushi and cafe latte. Swedish cuisine could be best described as centered around crisp and soft bread, cultured dairy products, fresh berries, cultured dairy products, stone fruits, beef, lamb, chicken, eggs, pork, and seafood. Potatoes are served as a side dish. Swedish cuisine embodies a great variety of bread made in different unique shapes and sizes, made out of wheat, rye, oat, sourdough or whole grain.

There are several sweetened bread types, and some are flavored with spices. Many meat dishes are available in Swedish cuisine like meatballs and stews. There are fruit soups like rosehip soup and blueberry soup served in this cuisine. Butter and margarine are the essential fat sources, though olive oil is also popular in the region. Sweden's pastry tradition offers a variety of cookies, yeast buns, biscuits, and cakes, and many of them are enjoyed with coffee and hot beverages.

Swedish *husmanskost* includes all the traditional Swedish meals that are made using the local ingredients, and it makes the everyday Swedish cuisine. The word "husmanskost" originated from "husman," which means "house owner." It was originally used for different kinds of simple countryside food. The real Swedish *husmanskost* made use of predominantly local food ingredients like pork in different forms, cereals, fish, potato, milk, cabbage, onions, root vegetables, apples, berries, etc. Beef and lamb were used more sparingly. Besides berries, apples are the most used traditional fruit, eaten fresh, or served as apple pie, applesauce, or apple cake.

Swedish Journey

L ocated on the Scandinavian peninsula, Sweden is the fifth largest country in Europe, and it shares its borders with Norway and Finland. The nation's shores line the Baltic Sea, and it has the Gulf of Bothnia, The Skagerrak, Oresund, and Kattegat straits. The Torner River passes through the border it shares with Finland in the east. The northern part of Sweden is situated near the Arctic Circle, and the southern part has maritime borders with Estonia, Latvia, Lithuania, Russia, Poland, Germany, and Denmark. With its 450 295 square kilometers of land, Sweden covers twice the bigger area than Great Britain. Due to the harsh climatic conditions, the majority of the population lives in the southern part of the country. Even its capital Stockholm is also located in the southern region. The Swedish language is a North Germanic language that has an influence from Norwegian and Danish. Whereas English is still a widely spoken language in the country.

Sweden has a rich history, and it's blessed with some amazing European landscapes that everyone must visit. The country is no less than a traveler's paradise. Its majestic lakes, the hidden forest, and organized urban areas attract hundreds of tourists every other day. My visit to Sweden delivered some of my most amazing experiences and memories. Before actually visiting the place, I was expecting to be full of snow-capped towns, but there was so much more to explore. Let's begin with the Vasa Museum, which I toured when I was in Stockholm. This museum has attracted more than twenty million tourists since 1990. The place is named after the Swedish Imperial fleet named Vasa battleship, which sank during its first trip in 1628. The museum takes you back in time and exhibits different items that were lost on that voyage.

Then there's the oldest open-air museum known as Skansen, which represents the timeline of the historic villages of Sweden from 1720 to the 1960s. There are open space churches, old mills, traditional houses, and classic schools to visit. The most captivating site in Sweden is an old town in Stockholm known as the Gamla Stan, which has Scandinavian-style houses painted with tempting and captivating colors. There are stone-paved paths and old-style lanes in these towns.

If you're fascinated by the palaces, then the fairytale Drottningholm Palace, a must-visit, is located on Lovo Island. The place is located 11 km away from Stockholm, and it takes 45 minutes to there by boat. This palace was originally built in the 17th century, and it's now the official residence of the Swedish royal family.

Additionally, it's interesting to mention here that Stockholm is often referred to as the Venice of North and mainly because the city is surrounded by islands that make Stockholm's archipelago. These islands have small summerhouse which is built with beautiful color and in traditional styles. These summerhouses are also a major attraction for tourists. There are stromma boats available on these islands where you can ride with your family to enjoy boating. In the north you can visit the Ice Hotel at Jukkasjarvi located in Kiruna; and then there's the Gota Canal that you must visit.

Breakfast

Cheese Pie

Preparation time: 10 minutes
Cook time: 30 minutes
Nutrition facts (per serving): 253 cal (22g fat, 21g protein, 4g fiber)

Add rich and delicious cheese pie for all that you need to make your dinner extra special. This one is made from traditional Swedish cheese and a cream filling.

Ingredients (6 servings)
Pie pastry
4 ½ oz. butter
2 cups wheat flour
1 tablespoon water

Filling
10 ½ oz. grated Västerbottensost cheese (or other hard cheese)
3 eggs
2 cups whipped cream
1 pinch black pepper

Preparation
At 400 degrees F, preheat your oven. Mix the flour with the butter in a food processor until crumbly. Stir in the water and mix well until it makes smooth dough. Spread this dough in a pie dish and prick it with a fork. Bake the dough for 10 minutes. Beat all eggs with cheese, cream, black pepper, and salt in a bowl. Add this cream cheese filling to the crust and bake for almost 20 minutes. Allow it to cool and then slice. Serve.

Swedish Rice Ring

Preparation time: 15 minutes
Cook time: 25 minutes
Nutrition facts (per serving): 170 cal (9g fat, 4g protein, 0g fiber)

This Swedish rice ring is one healthy breakfast that can be served with powdered sugar toppings and any fruit preserves.

Ingredients (6 servings)
2 envelopes of unflavored gelatin
¼ cup cold water
3 cups whole milk
½ cup uncooked long-grain rice
½ cup sugar
½ teaspoon salt
1 cup heavy whipping cream
Fresh or thawed (frozen) strawberries

Preparation
Mix cold water with gelatin in a small bowl and keep it aside. Mix salt, sugar, rice, and milk in a saucepan and cook for 20 minutes on a simmer until rice is soft. Stir in the gelatin mixture and mix until the mixture thickens. Beat the cream in a mixer until fluffy and, then add it to the rice. Mix well and spread the mixture into 6 cup Bundt pan greased with cooking spray. Cover and refrigerate for 3 hours. Garnish with berries and serve.

Swedish Pancakes

Preparation time: 10 minutes
Cook time: 15 minutes
Nutrition facts (per serving): 155 cal (8g fat, 13g protein, 2g fiber)

If you haven't tried the Swedish pancakes before, then here comes a simple and easy to cook recipe that you can recreate at home in no time with minimum efforts.

Ingredients (4 servings)
3 large eggs
2 cups of milk
1 cup unbleached all-purpose flour
6 tablespoons unsalted butter, melted
1 tablespoon granulated sugar
½ teaspoon pure vanilla extract
½ teaspoon salt
Confectioners' sugar, for garnish
Fruits (strawberries, raspberries, or sliced melon)
Jam, for garnish

Preparation
Beat all eggs with ½ cup milk in a bowl for 3 minutes. Stir in the flour and mix well until smooth. Add salt, vanilla, granulated sugar, butter, and the remaining milk. Next, mix well until smooth. Grease a skillet with cooking spray and place it over medium heat. Add a tablespoon of batter into the pan and cook the batter for 3 minutes per side. Cook the remaining Swedish pancakes in the same manner. Garnish with confectioner's sugar, jam, and fresh fruit. Serve.

Swedish Doughnuts

Preparation time: 15 minutes
Cook time: 20 minutes
Nutrition facts (per serving): 125 cal (2g fat, 3g protein, 1g fiber)

The Swedish Doughnuts are famous for their delicious flavor and fluffy texture. Made from flour and mashed potatoes, these doughnuts pair well with all types of egg omelets.

Ingredients (8 servings)

2 large eggs
1 cup of sugar
2 cups cold mashed potatoes
¾ cup buttermilk
2 tablespoons butter, melted
1 teaspoon vanilla extract
4 ½ cups all-purpose flour
4 teaspoons baking powder
1 teaspoon baking soda
1 teaspoon salt
2 teaspoons ground nutmeg
⅛ teaspoon ground ginger
Oil for deep frying
Sugar, to serve

Preparation

Beat all eggs with sugar in a large bowl. Stir in the vanilla, butter, buttermilk, and potatoes, and then mix well. Stir in the salt, ginger, nutmeg, salt, baking soda, baking powder, and flour, then mix well until it makes smooth dough. Cover this dough and refrigerate for 2 hours. Roll the dough on the floured working surface into ½ inch thickness. Cut 2 ½ inch round doughnuts using a cookie cutter. Deep fry the doughnuts in hot oil at 375 degrees F until golden brown.

Transfer the prepared doughnuts to a plate using a slotted spoon. Garnish the doughnuts with sugar. Serve.

Swedish Rye Bread

Preparation time: 10 minutes
Cook time: 35 minutes
Nutrition facts (per serving): 109 cal (2g fat, 2g protein, 1g fiber)

This Swedish rye bread is one of the most popular meals which taste heavenly when cooked and baked at home. Serve warm with your favorite toppings on the side.

Ingredients (8 servings)

1 package active dry yeast
1 ¾ cups warm water
¼ cup packed brown sugar
¼ cup molasses
2 tablespoons shortening
2 teaspoons salt
2 ½ cups rye flour
4 ¼ cups all-purpose flour
2 tablespoons butter, melted

Preparation

Mix ¼ cup water with yeast in a bowl and leave it for 5 minutes. Stir in the salt, shortening, molasses, sugar, and remaining water. Mix well and add the rye flour. Next, mix well until it makes smooth dough. Transfer the prepared dough to a floured surface and knead it for 8 minutes. Transfer the prepared dough to a greased bowl and cover it with a plastic sheet. Leave the dough for 2 hours, and then punch it down. Divide the dough into 4 pieces and shape them into a loaf. Place the prepared loaves on the baking sheet and cover. Leave the loaves for 45 minutes. Bake them for 35 minutes at 350 degrees F in the oven. Garnish with butter and serve.

Potato Pancakes

Preparation time: 15 minutes
Cook time: 10 minutes
Nutrition facts (per serving): 171 cal (7g fat, 3g protein, 2g fiber)

Try these potato pancakes for your breakfast, so you'll totally forget about the rest. The recipe is simple and gives you lots of nutrients in one place.

Ingredients (8 servings)
4 cups peeled potatoes, shredded
1 large egg, beaten
3 tablespoons all-purpose flour
1 tablespoon onion, grated
1 teaspoon salt
¼ teaspoon black pepper
Oil for frying
Chopped parsley
Applesauce, for topping
Sour cream, for topping

Preparation
Soak the shredded potatoes in cold water, drain, and then squeeze the excess water. Transfer the potatoes to a bowl. Stir in the black pepper, salt, onion, flour, and egg. Mix well and keep it aside. Set a skillet greased with ¼ inch oil over medium heat and drop ⅓ cup potato mixture, then sear for 5 minutes per side until golden brown. Cook the remaining pancakes in the same way. Serve.

Swedish Apple Pie

Preparation time: 10 minutes
Cook time: 30 minutes
Nutrition facts (per serving): 174 cal (7g fat, 5g protein, 2g fiber)

Here comes a classic dessert and a breakfast that will give you authentic Swedish flavors in one place.

Ingredients (6 servings)
½ cup sugar
¼ cup whole wheat flour
¼ cup all-purpose flour
1 teaspoon baking powder
½ teaspoon salt
½ teaspoon ground cinnamon
1 large egg
¼ teaspoon vanilla extract
2 tart apples, chopped
¾ cup walnuts, toasted and chopped
Confectioners' sugar

Preparation
Mix the sugar with salt, cinnamon, baking powder, and flours in a large bowl. Beat the egg with vanilla and pour into the flour mixture. Mix well until smooth. Stir in the walnuts and the apples and then spread this mixture on a 9-inch pie plate. Bake it for almost 30 minutes at 350 degrees F in the oven. Garnish with sugar and serve.

Swedish Creme

Preparation time: 15 minutes
Cook time: 10 minutes
Nutrition facts (per serving): 440 cal (32g fat, 4g protein, 1g fiber)

This Swedish crème is one of the Swedish specialties, and everyone must try this interesting combination of different creams and raspberries.

Ingredients (8 servings)
2 cups heavy whipping cream
1 cup sugar
1 envelope unflavored gelatin
1 teaspoon vanilla extract
1 teaspoon almond extract
2 cups sour cream
1 cup raspberries

Preparation
Mix the cream with 1 cup sugar in a large saucepan and cook on low heat until it reaches 160 degrees F. Add the gelatin and mix well until dissolved. Remove the prepared mixture from the heat and allow it to cool for 10 minutes. Add the sour cream, mix well, and divide the mixture into 8 serving bowls. Refrigerate for 1 hour and then garnish with sugar and berries. Serve.

Old-Fashioned Gingersnaps

Preparation time: 15 minutes
Cook time: 10 minutes
Nutrition facts (per serving): 150 cal (8g fat, 1g protein, 0g fiber)

These gingersnaps are the best way to enjoy earthy and sweet cookies in a savory style. Made from flour and molasses, they're a warming delight for your breakfast and snack.

Ingredients (24 servings)
¾ cup butter, softened
1 cup of sugar
1 large egg (room temperature)
¼ cup molasses
2 cups all-purpose flour
2 teaspoons baking soda
1 teaspoon ground cinnamon
1 teaspoon ground cloves
1 teaspoon ground ginger
¼ teaspoon salt

Preparation
Beat the softened butter with sugar in a bowl until fluffy. Stir in the molasses and the egg and then mix well. Add salt, ginger, cloves, cinnamon, baking soda, and flour, and then mix until smooth. Make 1 ¼ inch round balls from this mixture and coat them with sugar. Place the balls on baking sheets and press them into flat cookies. Bake for almost 10 minutes at 375 degrees F. Allow the cookies to cool and serve.

Saffron Buns

Preparation time: 15 minutes
Cook time: 3 hours 15 minutes
Nutrition facts (per serving): 312 cal (16g fat, 13g protein, 1g fiber)

The Swedish saffron buns are a delight to serve at the breakfast table. They're known for strong saffron flavors and the energizing combination of ingredients.

Ingredients (6 servings)

¾ cup milk
½ teaspoon saffron threads
13 teaspoon sugar
¼-ounce dry yeast
4 cups all-purpose flour
½ teaspoon salt
3 cardamom pods, ground
¼ cup unsalted butter, softened
¼ cup of sour cream
2 large eggs
Raisins
Glaze
1 egg, beaten

Preparation

Mix the milk with 1 teaspoon sugar and saffron in a small pot and heat it to 115 degrees F. Remove it from the heat, then add yeast, mix well, and leave it for 10 minutes. Stir in the flour, eggs, sour cream, butter, cardamom, salt, and remaining sugar, then mix well until it makes smooth dough. Knead this dough on a floured surface and transfer it to a greased bowl and cover. Leave this dough for 1 hour. Punch down the dough and roll it into 14 inches long rope. Curl this rope into an S shape and place it on a baking sheet. Cover and leave it for 30 minutes. Brush this bun with the egg wash and press the raisins on top of the bun. Bake the buns for 11 minutes in the oven at 400 degrees F. Serve.

Cardamom Sour Cream Waffles

Preparation time: 15 minutes
Cook time: 15 minutes
Nutrition facts (per serving): 235 cal (6g fat, 8g protein, 2g fiber)

If you haven't tried these cardamom waffles, then you must try now as they have no parallel in taste and texture.

Ingredients (7 servings)
¾ cup all-purpose flour
¾ cup whole wheat flour
1 ½ teaspoons baking powder
1 teaspoon ground cardamom
¾ teaspoon baking soda
½ teaspoon ground cinnamon
¼ teaspoon salt
2 large eggs
1 cup milk
¾ cup sour cream
½ cup packed brown sugar
1 tablespoon butter, melted
1 teaspoon vanilla extract

Preparation
Mix the flours with baking powder, cardamom, baking soda, cinnamon, salt, milk, eggs, sour cream, butter, and vanilla extract in a bowl until smooth. Pour ¼ cup batter into the waffle iron and cook until golden brown. Cook the remaining waffles and serve.

Cardamom Braid Bread

Preparation time: 5 minutes
Cook time: 25 minutes
Nutrition facts (per serving): 114 cal (3g fat, 3g protein, 1g fiber)

This braided cardamom braid is one of the most delicious breakfast on this menu to try. You can use different variations for its toppings.

Ingredients (10 servings)
6 cups all-purpose flour
2 packages active dry yeast
1 ½ teaspoon ground cardamom
1 teaspoon salt
1 ⅔ cup milk
½ cup butter, cubed
½ cup honey
2 large eggs
2 tablespoons sugar

Preparation
Mix the yeast, 2 cups flour, salt, and cardamom in a bowl. Mix the butter, honey, and 1 ½ cups milk in a saucepan. Cook the mixture until its temperature reaches 130 degrees F. Stir in the flour mixture and mix well until smooth. Add the remaining flour and stir until it makes smooth dough.

Transfer the prepared dough to a floured surface and knead it for 8 minutes. Place the dough in a greased bowl and cover it with a plastic sheet. Leave it for 45 minutes, and then punch it down. Cut the dough in half and divide each half into three portions. Shape each portion into a 14-inch rope. Pinch three dough ropes together at one end and braid them. Repeat the same with the remaining ropes. Place the braided bread on a baking sheet and cover it with a kitchen towel. Leave the bread for 30 minutes.

Mix the remaining milk with sugar in a bowl and brush it over the braided loaves. Bake the bread for 25 minutes at 375 degrees F. Allow the bread to cool. Serve.

Appetizers
and Snacks

Marinated Cheese
(Vaniljmarinerad Västerbottensost)

Preparation time: 15 minutes
Cook time: 10 minutes
Nutrition facts (per serving): 349 cal (3.6g fat, 22g protein, 5.4g fiber)

It's about time to try this classic and make it more diverse and flavorsome. Use this cheese to garnish your meals and snacks.

Ingredients (6 servings)
1 vanilla pod
½ cup of water
½ cup caster sugar
6 tablespoon Xanté (pear brandy)
4 oz. Västerbottensost, cut into pieces
Cocktail sticks for serving

Preparation
Add water, caster sugar, and vanilla seeds to a saucepan and cook over moderate heat for 10 minutes. Allow the mixture to cool; then add Xanté and mix well. Pour this mixture into a jar and refrigerate for 30 minutes. Slice and serve.

Caviar Kalix On Rye Bread (Kalix Löjrom På Rågbröd)

Preparation time: 10 minutes
Nutrition facts (per serving): 392 cal (19g fat, 25g protein, 2g fiber)

Caviar on rye bread is here to add flavors to your dinner table, but this time with a mix of caviar and sour cream. You can try it as an effortless meal to prepare in no time.

Ingredients (4 servings)
4 slices rye bread
Butter
¾ cup gräddfil or sour cream
½ red onion, chopped
Lemon juice
White pepper, to taste
7 oz. Kalix löjrom or other similar caviar
Dill, to garnish

Preparation
Cut each rye bread slice into a circle using a cookie cutter. Mix the red onion with gräddfil in a bowl. Divide this mixture on top of the bread rounds. Drizzle lemon juice and white pepper on top. Garnish with caviar and dill. Serve.

Asparagus Mousse with Prawns (Sparrismousse Med Räkor Med Dill)

Preparation time: 10 minutes
Cook time: 20 minutes
Nutrition facts (per serving): 471 cal (13g fat, 19g protein, 3g fiber)

Let's have a rich and delicious combination of asparagus mousse with prawns topping. Try it with warm bread slices, and you'll simply love it.

Ingredients (4 servings)

8 oz. green asparagus spears
2 gelatin sheets
4 tablespoon whipping cream
10 oz. prawns
1 tablespoon dill, chopped
Salt and white pepper to taste
1 lemon, zest only

Preparation

Boil the asparagus in salted water, drain, and keep the water aside. Puree the asparagus in the food processor until smooth. Soak the gelatin sheet for 5 minutes in a bowl filled with water and remove the excess water. Add 3 tablespoon of asparagus water to a saucepan and stir in gelatin. Cook until melted. Stir in the asparagus puree and mix well. Add the cream, prawns, salt, and black pepper. Cook for 4 minutes and then garnish with dill and lemon zest. Serve.

Cheese Palmier
(Västerbottensost Palmier)

Preparation time: 10 minutes
Cook time: 10 minutes
Nutrition facts (per serving): 472 cal (29g fat, 31g protein, 1.4g fiber)

Cheese palmier is the Swedish delights that you would never want to miss. They're here to make your meal special. You can always serve the cheese palmier with your favorite sauce.

Ingredients (6 servings)
6 oz. ready-made puff pastry
2 oz. Västerbottensost or similar hard cow cheese, grated
6 Swedish anchovies' fillets
1 egg, beaten

Preparation
At 425 degrees F, preheat your oven. Grease two baking sheets with cooking oil. Spread the pastry into an 8x12 inches sheet. Top this pastry with cheese and fold the pastry on top of the cheese to make a square. Roll the pastry into 8 x 8-inch square. Cut this square in half and place an anchovy fillet on top of each strip. Roll the pastry around the fillets and brush with egg. Place the palmier on a baking sheet and Bake for almost 10 minutes. Serve warm.

Cheese Tuiles

Preparation time: 15 minutes
Cook time: 10 minutes
Nutrition facts (per serving): 420 cal (13g fat, 44g protein, 2g fiber)

These cheese Tuiles taste amazing, and they're simple and easy to cook. They're truly great for all cheese and olive lovers.

Ingredients (8 servings)

4 oz. Västerbottensost or Parmesan cheese, grated
8 black olives, pitted, and halved

Preparation

Divide the grated cheese onto a baking sheet into 16 piles and place half of an olive at the center of each cheese pile. Bake the cheese for 10 minutes until golden brown. Serve.

Cheese With Olives

Preparation time: 15 minutes
Cook time: 15 minutes
Nutrition facts (per serving): 258 cal (6.4g fat, 29g protein, 1g fiber)

Cheese with olives is always an easy way to add extra nutrients to your menu, and here's something that you can make in just a few minutes.

Ingredients (8 servings)
12 green olives, pitted
3 oz. Västerbottensost or Parmesan cheese, grated
1 tablespoon butter, cut into small pieces
5 tablespoon all-purpose flour
1 tablespoon water
1 pinch of cayenne pepper
3 tablespoon sesame seeds

Preparation
At 400 degrees F, preheat your oven. Layer a baking sheet with parchment paper. Mix flour with water, butter, cheese, and cayenne pepper in a bowl until it makes a dough. Next, divide the dough into 12 pieces. Spread these pieces into a round and place one olive at the center of each round. Fold the dough around the olive and roll it into a ball. Coat the balls with the sesame seeds. Place the balls on a baking sheet and Bake for almost 15 minutes. Serve.

Shellfish on Rye Bread (Skaldjur På Rågbröd)

Preparation time: 15 minutes
Nutrition facts (per serving): 379 cal (13g fat, 25g protein, 3g fiber)

Here's a delicious and savory combination of shellfish and rye bread with cream fraiche that you must add to your menu.

Ingredients (2 servings)
6 tablespoon mayonnaise
6 tablespoon crème fraiche
1 tablespoon dill, chopped
1 lemon, juice, and zest
8 oz. shellfish, peeled
Salt and white pepper
2 slices of buttered rye bread
1 tablespoon chives, chopped
2 lemon slices cut into small wedges

Preparations
Mix the crème fraiche with mayonnaise and lemon zest in a bowl. Stir in the shellfish and mix well. Cut the bread into 16 pieces and spread the mayo mixture on top of each piece. Garnish with chives and lemon. Serve.

New Potatoes with Roe
(Nypotatis Med Rom)

Preparation time: 15 minutes
Cook time: 12 minutes
Nutrition facts (per serving): 244 cal (6g fat, 8g protein, 5g fiber)

If you haven't tried the Nypotatis med rom, then here comes a simple and easy to cook recipe that you can replicate on your own.

Ingredients (8 servings)
8 medium new potatoes
½ cup crème fraiche
2 oz. vendace roe
½ oz. chives

Preparation
Boil all the potatoes in salted water for 12 minutes, then drain. Cut the potatoes in half and chop them. Mix the crème fraiche and chives in a bowl. Add a dollop of this mixture on top of each potato half and garnish with roe and chives. Serve.

Filled Egg Halves (Fyllda Ägghalvor)

Preparation time: 15 minutes
Nutrition facts (per serving): 336 cal (13g fat,28g protein, 1.7g fiber)

A perfect mix of egg yolk and tabasco prawn filling inside the egg whites. Serve fresh with your favorite side salad for the best taste.

Ingredients (6 servings)
6 hard-boiled eggs
4 tablespoon crème fraiche
12 drops of tabasco
12 prawns
10 teaspoon Kalix löjrom or any salmon caviar
Letuce leaves
Black pepper, to taste
Cress or fresh herbs to garnish

Preparation
Peel the eggs and slice them in half. Remove the yolks from their whites and mash them in a bowl. Stir in the crème fraiche, tabasco, salt, and black pepper in a bowl. Add this mixture to a piping bag and pipe it into the egg whites. Garnish each egg white with a prawn and ½ teaspoon kalix löjrom. Garnish with herbs and serve.

Smoked Eel Canapés (Rökt Ål Kanapéer)

Preparation time: 15 minutes
Nutrition facts (per serving): 316 cal (7g fat, 24g protein, 12g fiber)

The Swedish smoked eel is famous for its unique taste and aroma, so now you can bring those exotic flavors home by using this recipe.

Ingredients (4 servings)
½ red onion, chopped
1 tablespoon white wine vinegar
1 teaspoon granulated sugar
16 pieces knäckebröd, diced
4 slices of smoked eel
Black pepper, to taste
3 tablespoon crème fraîche
Herbs for garnish

Preparation
Mix the onion with sugar and vinegar in a bowl and leave it for ½ an hour. Top each knackered piece with 1 piece of eel and garnish each with onion, black pepper, crème fraiche, and herbs. Serve.

Egg and Anchovies on Crispbread (Gubbröra)

Preparation time: 10 minutes
Nutrition facts (per serving): 343 cal (13g fat, 15g protein, 2g fiber)

Gubbröra has an interesting name and a unique combination of ingredients as well. It offers a mix of crispbread and anchovies' toppings.

Ingredients (6 servings)
6 hard-boiled eggs, chopped
2 egg yolks
2 tablespoon red onion, chopped
2 tablespoon chives, chopped
¼ cup dill, chopped
6 anchovies in oil,
1 tablespoon anchovy oil
4 slices crispbread
Lime or lemon halves, to serve

Preparation
Mix the chopped eggs with white pepper, anchovy oil, anchovies, dill, chives, onion, and egg yolks in a bowl. Divide this mixture over the crispbread and garnish with lime halves and dill. Serve.

Salads

Apple, Celery and Walnut Salad

Preparation time: 15 minutes
Nutrition facts (per serving): 441 cal (11g fat, 34g protein, 5g fiber)

This apple and celery salad is cherished by all, young and adult. It's simple and quick to make. This delight is great to serve at dinner tables.

Ingredients (4 servings)

6 celery sticks, chopped
3 apples, cored and diced
4 oz. white grapes, diced
1 handful of walnut pieces
2 tablespoon olive oil
3 tablespoon apple cider vinegar
2 teaspoons of any clear honey
Salt and black pepper, to taste

Preparation

Toss all the apple celery salad ingredients together in a bowl and serve.

Beetroot and Apple Salad (Rödbetssallad Med Äpple)

Preparation time: 5 minutes
Nutrition facts (per serving): 470 cal (28g fat, 6g protein, 1.7g fiber)

Try the beetroot and apple salad at the dinner as it's infused with an amazing blend of apple cider vinegar and walnuts.

Ingredients (4 servings)
2 beetroot bulbs, chopped
1 tablespoon apple cider vinegar
1½ tablespoon walnut oil
¼ teaspoon sea salt
Black pepper, to taste
2 medium apples
1 tablespoon chervil, chopped
2 tablespoon walnut pieces
2 tablespoon crème fraiche
2 teaspoon horseradish, grated
2 small sprigs of chervil

Preparation
Toss all the beetroot apple salad ingredients together in a bowl and serve.

Beetroot Salad with Feta Cheese (Rödbetssallad Med Fetaost)

Preparation time: 5 minutes
Cook time: 5 minutes
Nutrition facts (per serving): 205 cal (11.8g fat, 10g protein, 2g fiber)

This beetroot salad is a typical Swedish side meal, which is a must on the Swedish menu. It has a rich mix of beetroot and cheese.

Ingredients (4 servings)

5 oz. raw beetroot, peeled
1 teaspoon butter
1 tablespoon olive oil
1 teaspoon caraway seeds
1 teaspoon sesame seeds
1 lemon, zest, and juice
Salt and black pepper, to taste
4 oz. feta cheese, crumbled
1 tablespoon herbs, chopped

Preparation

Sauté the sesame seeds and caraway with butter and olive oil in a skillet for 2 minutes. Stir in the grated beetroot and sauté for 3 minutes. Remove this beetroot mixture from the heat and add black pepper, salt, lemon juice, and zest. Mix well and transfer to a salad bowl. Toss in the herbs and remaining cheese. Serve.

Classic Beetroot Salad (Klassisk Rödbetssallad)

Preparation time: 5 minutes
Nutrition facts (per serving): 520 cal (32g fat, 43g protein, 0g fiber)

Simple and easy to make, this recipe is a must to try on this menu. Classic Beetroot salad is a delight for the dinner table.

Ingredients (4 servings)
12 oz. pickled beetroot, drained and diced
1 small tart apple, cored and diced
3 tablespoon mayonnaise
3 tablespoon crème fraiche
1 dash balsamic vinegar
¼ teaspoon lemon juice
Salt and black pepper, to taste
1 tablespoon chopped chives

Preparation
Mix the mayonnaise with crème fraiche, balsamic vinegar, lemon juice, salt, black pepper, and chopped chives in a bowl. Stir in the beetroot and apple. Mix well and serve.

Honey-Glazed Beetroot (Honungsglaserade Rödbetor)

Preparation time: 5 minutes
Cook time: 1 hour 45 minutes
Nutrition facts (per serving): 445 cal (21g fat, 60g protein, 4g fiber)

Swedish honey glazed beetroot salad is one of the traditional Swedish side meals that's served along with every entrée.

Ingredients (4 servings)
1 ¼ lb. beetroot
4 tablespoon water
4 tablespoon apple cider vinegar
4 tablespoon honey
Salt and black pepper, to taste
1 tablespoon parsley, chopped

Preparation
At 350 degrees F, preheat your oven. Add beetroots and 4 tablespoon water to a roasting pan and cover with an aluminum foil. Bake them for 90 minutes and, then slice them into wedges. Boil vinegar in a saucepan, then add beetroot wedges and cook for 5 minutes. Add honey and cook for 10 minutes. Stir in the black pepper and salt. Mix well and garnish with parsley. Serve.

Carrot and Raisin Salad
(Morot- Och Russin Salad)

Preparation time: 5 minutes
Nutrition facts (per serving): 361 cal (20g fat, 11g protein, 0.8g fiber)

A perfect mix of carrot, mayonnaise, and raisins is all that you need to expand your Swedish menu. Simple and easy to make, this recipe is a must to try.

Ingredients (4 servings)
8 oz. carrots, shredded
3 ½ oz. raisins
2 tablespoon mayonnaise
2 teaspoon caster sugar
1 tablespoon milk

Preparation
Toss all the carrot raisins salad ingredients together in a bowl and serve.

Celeriac Purée
(Rotselleripuré)

Preparation time: 15 minutes
Cook time: 20 minutes
Nutrition facts (per serving): 325 cal (20g fat, 6g protein, 2g fiber)

Do you want to enjoy celeriac with a Swedish twist? Then try this Swedish Celeriac puree recipe. You can serve it as your favorite dip.

Ingredients (4 servings)
1 ¼ lb. celeriac, peeled and diced
2 cups of milk
4 tablespoon whipping cream
2 tablespoon butter
½ teaspoon salt
Black pepper, to taste
Freshly grated nutmeg

Preparation
Boil the celeriac with milk in a saucepan and reduce its heat. Cook for 20 minutes until soft. Drain and transfer the celeriac to a bowl. Keep the milk aside. Puree the celeriac and transfer to a bowl. Stir in the milk, cream, butter, salt, black pepper, and nutmeg. Mix well and serve.

Pickled Chanterelle Mushrooms (Syltade Kantareller)

Preparation time: 15 minutes
Cook time: 15 minutes
Nutrition facts (per serving): 624 cal (29g fat, 72g protein, 2g fiber)

The classic chanterelle mushrooms recipe is here to complete your Swedish menu. This meal can be served on all special occasions and festive celebrations.

Ingredients (4 servings)
4 cups wild mushrooms
1 tablespoon lemon juice
1 shallot, peeled and sliced
2 cups white vinegar
½ cup caster sugar
⅛ inch fresh ginger, peeled and sliced
1 small cinnamon stick
2 cloves
1 teaspoon salt

Preparation
Add the mushrooms with the shallots, lemon juice, and salt to a saucepan. Cook this mixture for almost 10 minutes, then add cinnamon, ginger, sugar, and vinegar, and cook for 5 minutes. Add this mixture to a sterilized jar and cover its lid. Cover and keep the jar for 3 weeks in a dark place. Serve.

Pickled Cucumber (Smörgåsgurka)

Preparation time: 15 minutes
Cook time: 10 minutes
Nutrition facts (per serving): 423 cal (6g fat, 38g protein, 0g fiber)

The pickled cucumber is one popular side meal on the Swedish menu that you must serve at the festive celebration. This recipe will add a lot of appeal and color to your dinner table.

Ingredients (4 servings)
2 lbs. pickling cucumbers
4 ¼ cups water
¾ cup of salt

Pickling solution
1¾ cups granulated sugar
¾ cup of water
¾ cup distilled malt vinegar
½ tablespoon yellow mustard seeds
1 teaspoon white peppercorns
12 small dill crowns
½ oz. horseradish, sliced
2 small blades of mace

Preparation
Mix the salt with water in a bowl, soak the cucumbers for 24 hours, and then drain. Add water, sugar, and vinegar to a saucepan and let it boil. Allow the mixture to cool. Add the sliced cucumbers to a mason jar. Pour this mixture into the cucumbers and top it with the remaining ingredients. Cover and keep the jar for 3 weeks in a dark place. Serve.

Fresh Cucumber with Dill (Färsk Gurka Med Dill)

Preparation time: 15 minutes
Nutrition facts (per serving): 378 cal (11g fat, 33g protein, 1.2g fiber)

These fresh cucumbers with dill are here to complete your Swedish menu. Add this salad to increase the fiber content of your meal.

Ingredients (2 servings)
1 cucumber
2 tablespoon sugar
2 tablespoon dill, chopped
2 tablespoon white wine vinegar
Salt and black pepper, to taste

Preparation
Place the cucumbers in a colander and drizzle salt on top. Leave them for 10 minutes. Rinse the cucumber and pat it dry. Mix sugar with water, black pepper, vinegar, and dill in a bowl. Stir in the cucumbers, mix, and serve.

Cheese Herb Potato Fans

Preparation time: 10 minutes
Cook time: 60 minutes
Nutrition facts (per serving): 318 cal (15g fat, 8g protein, 4g fiber)

Ingredients (8 servings)
8 medium potatoes
½ cup butter, melted
2 teaspoons salt
½ teaspoon pepper
⅔ cup cheddar cheese, shredded
⅓ cup Parmesan cheese, shredded
2 tablespoons minced fresh chives

Preparation
At 425 degrees F, preheat your oven. Make ⅛-inch-deep slices in each potato while leaving its base intact. Place the potatoes on a baking dish and drizzle butter, black pepper, and salt on top. Bake the potatoes for 55 minutes in the oven. Mix the cheese with the herbs and drizzle over the potatoes. Bake the potatoes for 5 minutes in the oven. Serve.

Soups

Rosehip soup (Nyponsoppa)

Preparation time: 10 minutes
Cook time: 35 minutes
Nutrition facts (per serving): 425 cal (17g fat, 5g protein, 0.8g fiber)

This Swedish rosehip soup will leave you spellbound due to its mildly sweet taste and the combination of rosehips with sugar.

Ingredients (8 servings)
4 cups fresh rosehips, seeds removed
8 cups of water
½ cup caster sugar
1 tablespoon corn flour

Preparation
Add the rosehip, water, and caster sugar to a saucepan and cook until mushy. Stir in the corn flour, mix, and cook until it thickens. Serve.

Nettle Soup

Preparation time: 10 minutes
Cook time: 30 minutes
Nutrition facts (per serving): 279 cal (16g fat, 5g protein, 3g fiber)

This classic nettle soup is one of the popular Swedish entrées that has a lot of nutritious ingredients to offer, including potatoes and nettle tops.

Ingredients (4 servings)
½ large nettle tops
Salt, to taste
1 tablespoon olive oil
1 teaspoon butter
½ cup shallots, chopped
½ cup celery, chopped
1-pound Yukon Gold, peeled and chopped
4 cups chicken stock
2 cups of water
1 bay leaf
1 teaspoon dried thyme
Black pepper, to taste
1 ½ tablespoons lemon juice
3 tablespoons of heavy whipping cream

Preparation
Boil water in a large pot and blanch the nettles in this water for 2 minutes. Transfer the nettles to a colander and strain. Sauté the celery with shallots, olive oil, and butter in a saucepan for 5 minutes. Stir in the potatoes, stock, thyme, bay leaf, one teaspoon salt, and cook for 5 minutes on a simmer. Add the blanched nettles and pour in 2 cups of water. Cook for 15 minutes on a simmer until potatoes are soft. Discard the bay leaves and puree the soup until smooth.

Add salt, lemon juice, and seasonings. Mix well and garnish with mint and black pepper. Serve.

Chicken Soup

Preparation time: 7 minutes
Cook time: 60 minutes
Nutrition facts (per serving): 376 cal (14g fat, 22g protein, 18g fiber)

This Swedish chicken soup recipe will make your day with a delightful taste. Serve warm with your favorite bread.

Ingredients (6 servings)
1 chicken with skin, cut into pieces
1 chopped onion, chopped
1 tomato, chopped
½ head of cabbage, diced
½ head of cauliflower, diced
1 bunch of parsley
6 ½ cup water
10 peppercorns
1 bay leaf
Salt to taste
4 garlic cloves
1 green chili pepper

Preparation
Add the chicken and rest of the ingredients to a cooking pot, cover, and cook for almost 60 minutes on a simmer. Garnish with parsley. Serve warm.

Cream of Mushroom Soup

Preparation time: 15 minutes
Cook time: 17 minutes
Nutrition facts (per serving): 136 cal (8g fat, 4g protein, 1g fiber)

Cream of mushroom soup is another nutritious yet simple meal for the table. It brings lots of nutrients and fibers to the table, along with healthy ingredients that are cooked together in a tempting combination.

Ingredients (6 servings)

2 tablespoons butter
½ pound fresh mushrooms, sliced
¼ cup chopped onion
6 tablespoons all-purpose flour
½ teaspoon salt
⅛ teaspoon black pepper
2 cans (14 ½ ounces) chicken broth
1 cup half-and-half cream

Preparation

Sauté the mushrooms and the onion with butter in a large saucepan until soft. Stir in the black pepper, salt, flour, and 1 can broth. Mix well until smooth. Stir in the mushroom mixture and the remaining broth. Boil the mixture and cook for 2 minutes until the mixture thickens. Reduce its heat and add the cream. Cook for 15 minutes on a simmer with occasional stirring. Serve warm.

Main Dishes

Grandma's Swedish Meatballs

Preparation time: 10 minutes
Cook time: 8 minutes
Nutrition facts (per serving): 348 cal (21g fat, 21g protein, 1g fiber)

If you can't think of anything to cook and make in a short time, then try this Swedish meatball recipe because it has great taste and texture to serve at the table.

Ingredients (8 servings)

1 large egg, beaten
½ cup crushed crackers
¼ teaspoon seasoned salt
¼ teaspoon pepper
½ pound ground beef
½ pound bulk pork sausage
⅓ cup all-purpose flour
2 ½ cups beef broth
Hot mashed potatoes
Minced fresh parsley

Preparation

Mix the egg with crackers, seasoned salt, black pepper, beef, and sausage in a bowl. Make 1-inch balls out of this mixture and coat the meatballs with ¼ cup flour. Sear the meatballs in a skillet greased with cooking oil. Pour in 2 cups broth and cook the mixture to boil. Reduce the heat and cover to cook for 6 minutes. Transfer the meatballs to a plate using a slotted spoon. Stir in remaining flour and broth, and then mix well until smooth. Cook this mixture on a boil for 2 minutes. Return the meatballs to the gravy and mix well. Garnish with parsley and serve warm.

Swedish Meatballs with Lingonberries

Preparation time: 10 minutes
Cook time: 15 minutes
Nutrition facts (per serving): 36 cal (2g fat, 3g protein, 2g fiber)

Here comes another Swedish meatball recipe, but this time with the twist of breadcrumbs and lingonberries, which make them super unique and exotic in taste and texture.

Ingredients (8 servings)
1 ⅔ cup evaporated milk
⅔ cup chopped onion
¼ cup fine dry breadcrumbs
½ teaspoon salt
½ teaspoon allspice
1 dash black pepper
1-pound lean ground beef
2 teaspoons butter
2 teaspoons beef bouillon granules
1 cup boiling water
½ cup cold water
2 tablespoons all-purpose flour
1 tablespoon lemon juice
Canned lingonberries, to taste

Preparation
Mix a ⅔ cup evaporated milk with the onion, breadcrumbs, salt, allspice, and black pepper in a bowl. Stir in the beef and mix well. Cover and refrigerate this prepared mixture for 30 minutes. Make 1-inch round balls from this mixture. Sear the meatballs in a greased skillet over medium heat until golden brown. Mix the bouillon with boiling water in a bowl and pour over the meatballs. Cover and cook for 15 minutes on a simmer. Mix the flour with cold water in a bowl,

pour the mixture into the skillet, and then add evaporated milk. Mix and cook until the mixture thickens. Serve warm with lingonberries. Enjoy.

Meatballs with Noodles

Preparation time: 15 minutes
Cook time: 40 minutes
Nutrition facts (per serving): 837 cal (33g fat, 50g protein, 4g fiber)

Have you tried these gravy-soaked meatballs with noodles? Well, here's a Swedish delight that gives you a fancy combination of meatballs with sauce and pasta.

Ingredients (8 servings)
¾ cup seasoned breadcrumbs
1 medium onion, chopped
2 large eggs, beaten
⅓ cup fresh parsley, minced
1 teaspoon black pepper
¾ teaspoon salt
2 pounds ground beef

Gravy
½ cup all-purpose flour
2-¾ cups milk
2 cans (10 ½ ounces) condensed beef consommé
1 tablespoon Worcestershire sauce
1 teaspoon black pepper
¾ teaspoon salt

Noodles
1 package (16 ounces) egg noodles
¼ cup butter, cubed
¼ cup fresh parsley, minced

Preparation

Mix the beef with the breadcrumbs, onion, eggs, parsley, ground black pepper, and salt in a bowl. Make 1 ½ inch round balls and sauté the meatballs in a greased skillet until brown. Transfer them to a plate lined with a paper towel. Add the flour to the same skillet and stir cook for 2-3 minutes until golden brown. Add the milk, salt, black pepper, Worcestershire sauce, and consommé. Mix well and cook for 2 minutes until the gravy thickens. Add the meatballs and cook for 20 minutes on a low simmer. Boil the noodles as per the package's instructions and add to the meatball mixture. Garnish with parsley. Serve warm.

Swedish Lard Sausage (Isterband)

Preparation time: 15 minutes
Cook time: 1 hr. 10 minutes
Nutrition facts (per serving): 181 cal (5g fat, 7g protein, 6g fiber)

If you haven't tried the Swedish lard sausages before, then here comes a simple and easy to cook recipe that you can recreate at home in no time with minimum efforts.

Ingredients (6 servings)
1 ½ cups barley groats
2 quarts beef stock
2 lbs. lean pork
2 lbs. lard
2 tablespoons salt
½ teaspoon white pepper
½ teaspoon ground ginger
20 feet hog casings

Preparation
Soak the barley in water overnight in a saucepan and cook the barley for 1 hour over medium heat. Strain the barley. Mix the barley with spices, seasoning, lard and pork, and ginger in a bowl. Stuff the casings with the sausage mixture. Tie both the ends of sausages and refrigerate them for 3 hours. Sear the sausage in a greased skillet until brown from both sides. Serve warm.

Sausage with Macaroni (Falukorv Med Makaroner)

Preparation time: 10 minutes
Cook time: 18 minutes
Nutrition facts (per serving): 350 cal (17g fat, 11g protein, 1g fiber)

Try this sausage with macaroni with your favorite herbs on top. Adding a dollop of cream or yogurt will make it even richer in taste.

Ingredients (6 servings)
3 ¼ pound macaroni pasta
1-pound Falukorv sausage, diced
2 tablespoons butter
Ketchup, for serving

Preparation
Boil the macaroni in water for 8 minutes in a saucepan and drain. Slice and sauté the sausages in a skillet with butter until golden brown. Add the sausage to the macaroni and mix well. Garnish with ketchup. Serve.

Stuffed Cabbage Rolls (Kåldomar)

Preparation time: 10 minutes
Cook time: 55 minutes
Nutrition facts (per serving): 127 cal (4g fat, 6g protein, 2g fiber)

Enjoy these stuffed cabbage rolls filled with rice filling. These cabbage rolls are great for those who are cutting down on their carb intake.

Ingredients (6 servings)
3 oz. long-grain rice
1 cup milk
2 Savoy cabbages
4 tablespoon butter
1 large onion, finely chopped
6 oz. pork mince
6 oz. beef mince
½ teaspoon fresh thyme, chopped
1 egg, beaten
Salt and black pepper, to taste
3 tablespoon golden light syrup

Preparation
Cook the rice with milk in a saucepan until soft, and then fluff it up. Divide the cabbage into leaves; blanch these leaves in boiling water for 1 minute, and then drain. Sauté the onion with 1 tablespoon butter in a skillet until soft. Mix the rice with fried onion, seasoning, beaten egg, thyme, pork, and beef, and then mix well. At 400 degrees F, preheat your oven. Add 2 tablespoon of the rice stuffing at the center of each blanched leaf and wrap the leaves around their fillings. Place the cabbage wraps in the casserole dish and pour the golden syrup and remaining butter on top. Bake these rolls for 40 minutes. Serve warm.

Baked Brill (Ugnsbakad Slättvar)

Preparation time: 10 minutes
Cook time: 50 minutes
Nutrition facts (per serving): 110 cal (11g fat, 22g protein, 6g fiber)

Make this baked brill in no time and enjoy it with some garnish on top. Adding juicy cucumber on top makes it super tasty.

Ingredients (2 servings)
1 whole brill, cleaned
2 tablespoon butter
2 tablespoon horseradish, grated
lemon wedges
Dill sprigs

Preparation
At 210 degrees F, preheat your oven. Brush the whole brill with butter and place it in a roasting pan. Roast the fish for 50 minutes and flip it once cooked halfway through. Garnish with horseradish, lemon wedges, and dill sprigs. Serve.

Sailor's Beef (Sjömansbiff)

Preparation time: 15 minutes
Cook time: 80 minutes
Nutrition facts (per serving): 336 cal (2g fat, 33 protein, 12g fiber)

This classic is quite famous in the southern region of Sweden; in fact, and it is a must to try because of its nutritional content.

Ingredients (4 servings)
1 ¼ lb. stewing steak, sliced
1 ¾ lb. waxy potatoes, peeled and sliced
¾ lb. onions, sliced
2 tablespoon butter
Salt and white pepper, to taste
10 oz. beer
1 cup beef stock
2 bay leaves
Parsley to garnish

Preparation
Pound the beef slices and dice them. Sauté the beef with butter in a skillet until brown. Transfer the beef to a plate. Stir in the butter and onion and sauté for 10 minutes. Add the beef, potatoes, bay leaves, beer, stock, and seasoning, and then boil. Cover and cook the mixture for 60 minutes on low heat. Garnish with parsley and serve warm.

Beef Stroganoff

Preparation time: 10 minutes
Cook time: 25 minutes
Nutrition facts (per serving): 367 cal (8g fat, 27g protein, 3g fiber)

This beef stroganoff is everything I was looking for. The beef, sour cream, and mushrooms make a complete package for a health enthusiast like I am!

Ingredients (4 servings)
9 oz. beef, sliced
3 tablespoon butter
1 small onion, peeled and sliced
¼ teaspoon nutmeg
Salt and black pepper, to taste
7 oz. mixed wild mushrooms, sliced
½ cup sour cream
1 tablespoon brandy or sherry

Preparation
Sauté the beef strips in a tablespoon of butter in a cooking pan until brown. Season the beef with black pepper and salt, and then transfer to a plate. Sauté the onions with a tablespoon butter in a saucepan until soft. And transfer the onions to the beef. Sauté the mushrooms with remaining butter in the same skillet for 4 minutes. Add the black pepper, salt, and nutmeg, and then reduce the heat to low. Add the sour cream and cook the mixture to a boil. Add the onions, beef, black pepper, and salt. Add the brandy and mix well. Serve warm.

Steak on A Plank (Plankstek)

Preparation time: 15 minutes
Cook time: 30 minutes
Nutrition facts (per serving): 386 cal (3g fat, 24g protein, 5g fiber)

This steak on a plank meal is so satisfying and makes a great serving. The steaks are served with potatoes and fresh veggies on the side.

Ingredients (4 servings)
4 (6 oz.) sirloin steaks
Salt and black pepper, to taste
1 tablespoon oil, for frying
1 tablespoon butter, for frying
1 ¾ lb. Duchess potatoes
8 oz. asparagus spears, blanched
8 slices of unsmoked streaky bacon
Béarnaise sauce, lightly warmed
8 cherry tomatoes, halved
Tarragon, to garnish

Preparation
Rub the steaks with black pepper. Preheat your broiler at 450 degrees F. Pipe the Duchess potatoes on a roasting plank. Spread the asparagus, cherry tomatoes, and bacon around steaks. Broil the potatoes for 12 minutes in the preheated broiler. Season the steaks with salt and sear them with oil and butter in a skillet for 2 minutes per side. Place the steak on the plank and roast for 12 minutes in the broiler. Pour the bearnaise sauce on top and garnish with tarragon. Serve warm.

Swedish Beef Burgers (Biff À La Lindström)

Preparation time: 15 minutes
Cook time: 25 minutes
Nutrition facts (per serving): 482 cal (4g fat, 28g protein, 3g fiber)

If you haven't tried the Swedish beef burgers before, then here comes a simple and easy to cook recipe to dazzle guests in no time with minimum efforts.

Ingredients (4 servings)
1 lb. minced beef
2 egg yolks
4 oz. onion, chopped
2 tablespoon pickled beetroot, chopped
2 tablespoon capers, chopped
2 tablespoon water
Salt and black pepper, to taste
1 tablespoon chives, chopped
2 tablespoon oil, for frying

Preparation
Mix the minced beef with chives, seasoning, water, beetroot, capers, onion, and egg yolks in a large bowl. Make four patties from this mixture and sear the burgers in a greased frying pan until golden brown from both sides. Serve warm.

Asparagus and Smoked Salmon Tart (Sparrispaj Med Rökt Lax)

Preparation time: 15 minutes
Cook time: 35 minutes
Nutrition facts (per serving): 358 cal (14g fat, 9g protein, 4g fiber)

You can give this salmon tart a try because it has a good and delicious combination of cheese, asparagus, and salmon.

Ingredients (4 servings)
9 oz. chilled puff pastry, thawed
2 eggs, beaten
7 oz. light Philadelphia cheese
2 tablespoon dill, chopped
2 tablespoon chives, chopped
White pepper, to taste
1 lb. green asparagus spears, trimmed
Olive oil
7 oz. smoked salmon, sliced

Preparation
At 400 degrees F, preheat your oven. Spread the puff pastry and layer the baking sheet with parchment paper. Place the pastry on the baking sheet. Brush the top with beaten egg and bake for almost 10 minutes until golden brown. Mix the egg with the chives, dill, cheese, and white pepper in a bowl. Sauté the asparagus with olive oil in a skillet until soft. Place the smoked salmon in the pastry and pour the cheese mixture on top. Add the sautéed asparagus on top. Bake for almost 25 minutes in the oven. Serve warm.

Lamb Stew with Dill Sauce (Dillkött)

Preparation time: 15 minutes
Cook time: 1 hour 30 minutes
Nutrition facts (per serving): 386 cal (11g fat, 32g protein, 3g fiber)

This lamb stew with dill sauce is a must-have for every fancy dinner; and with the help of this recipe, you can cook it in no time.

Ingredients (4 servings)

1 ¼ lb. lamb, neck fillet, cubed
1 onion, chopped
1 carrot, sliced
1 leek, sliced
1 bay leaf
1 sprig of fresh thyme
10 white peppercorns
1 teaspoon salt

Dill sauce

2 oz. fresh dill, chopped
½ cup of water
5 white peppercorns
¼ cup of sugar
3 tablespoon white vinegar
½ cup whipping cream
3 tablespoon corn flour, mixed with water

Preparation

Add the cold water and meat to a saucepan, boil, and then remove it from the heat. Drain and rinse the meat. Add the meat, onion, white peppercorns, salt, thyme, bay leaf, leek, and carrot to the saucepan and pour in enough water to cover the meat. Cook on a simmer for 60 minutes. Meanwhile, mix dill with water, vinegar, sugar, and peppercorn in a saucepan and cook for 5 minutes.

Strain the meat and vegetable and reserve 2 cups of broth. Return this broth to the saucepan. Add the cream and cook the broth mixture to a boil. Add the meat, vegetables, and dill reduction. Adjust the seasoning with salt and black pepper. Mix the corn flour with a tablespoon of water in a bowl and pour into the pan. Cook until the stew thickens. Serve warm.

Fried Herring (Stekt Strömming)

Preparation time: 15 minutes
Cook time: 14 minutes
Nutrition facts (per serving): 428 cal (17g fat, 11g protein, 8g fiber)

The refreshing fried herring always tastes great when you cook it with rye flour coating; it gets a fine crisp and a perfect color.

Ingredients (4 servings)
4 herring, filleted
2 tablespoon rye flour
Salt and white pepper to taste
2 tablespoon butter

Preparation
Rub the white pepper and salt over the herring fillets. Coat the herring with rye flour. Set a skillet with butter over medium heat. Sear the coated herring for 5-7 minutes per side until golden brown. Serve warm.

Game Stew (Viltgryta)

Preparation time: 15 minutes
Cook time: 75 minutes
Nutrition facts (per serving): 342 cal (17g fat, 38g protein, 0g fiber)

Are you in the mood to have a game stew on the Swedish menu? Well, you can serve this stew with a mix of veggies and rice.

Ingredients (4 servings)
¾ oz. dried wild mushrooms
2 tablespoon butter
1 ¼ lb. diced game
8 small shallots, peeled and halved
Salt and black pepper, to taste
4 juniper berries, crushed
2 tablespoon gin
½ cup whipped cream
8 oz. carrots, peeled and sliced

Preparation
Soak the mushrooms in a bowl filled with 1 cup cold water for 30 minutes. Strain the mushrooms and reserve their liquid. Sauté the meat with butter in a large pan over medium heat, then transfer to a plate. Sauté the onions in the same skillet and add the seasonings and berries. Add the mushrooms, their liquid, and the meat to the pan and mix well. Stir in the cream and the gin and cover to cook for 60 minutes on a simmer. Add the carrots and cook for 5 minutes. Serve warm.

Egg Cake (Skånsk Äggakaga)

Preparation time: 10 minutes
Cook time: 25 minutes
Nutrition facts (per serving): 425 cal (28g fat, 33g protein, 2g fiber)

Have you tried the Swedish egg cake before? Well, now you can enjoy this unique and flavorsome combination recipe at home.

Ingredients (8 servings)
1 ¼ lb. unsmoked bacon
1 ¼ cups all-purpose flour
1 ½ teaspoon salt
3 cups of milk
8 eggs
3 tablespoon butter
1 cup rårörda lingon

Preparation
Sauté the bacon in a skillet until crispy and then transfer to a plate lined with a paper towel. Mix the flour with half of the milk and salt in a bowl until smooth. Stir in the eggs and the remaining butter. Melt 2 tablespoon butter in a suitable frying pan and pour the batter into the skillet. Cook until set, flip the egg cake, and cook until golden brown. Serve with lingon on top.

Duck Breast with Lingonberry Sauce (Ankbröst Med Lingonsås)

Preparation time: 15 minutes
Cook time: 23 minutes
Nutrition facts (per serving): 443 cal (16g fat, 23g protein, 0.6g fiber)

These duck breasts with lingonberry sauce are always served as a complete meal; and this one, in particular, is great to have on a nutritious diet.

Ingredients (4 servings)
4 (6 oz.) duck breasts
Salt and black pepper, to taste
3 tablespoon caster sugar
2 tablespoon balsamic vinegar
1 ½ cups water
¼ cup chicken stock
6 oz. lingonberries
2 teaspoon corn flour
1 tablespoon butter

Preparation
Score the duck breasts and rub them with black pepper and salt. Marinate them for 30 minutes. At 425 degrees F, preheat your oven. Sear the duck breast in a skillet for 4 minutes per side until golden. Place the duck breasts on a trivet, place in a roasting pan. Roast them for 10 minutes. Meanwhile, add the sugar in a saucepan over medium-low heat. Stir in the water, chicken stock, and half of the lingo berries and then mix well. Cook for 5 minutes, and then stir in the corn flour. Strain the sauce through a sieve and return the mixture to the saucepan. Stir in the corn flour, mix well, and cook until the mixture thickens. Stir in the remaining lingo berries and mix well. Serve the duck breasts with lingonberry sauce on top. Garnish with butter and then serve warm.

Pasta with Crayfish (Pasta Med Kräftor)

Preparation time: 15 minutes
Cook time: 25 minutes
Nutrition facts (per serving): 338 cal (20g fat, 13g protein, 3g fiber)

Now you can quickly make a flavorsome pasta with crayfish and serve as a fancy meal for yourself and your guest.

Ingredients (4 servings)
6 oz. dried pasta
1 small onion, sliced
1 tablespoon butter
1 teaspoon corn flour
¼ cup white wine
¾ cup half-fat crème fraiche
1 lemon, grated zest
Salt and white pepper to taste
6 oz. packet of crayfish tails
2 tablespoon dill, chopped
½ lemon, quartered
2 small sprigs of dill for garnish

Preparation
Boil the pasta in a saucepan filled with boiling water according to the package's instruction and then drain. Sauté the onion with butter in a skillet for 5 minutes. Stir in the corn flour, wine, and crème fraiche. Next, mix well. Cook for 5 minutes, and then add lemon juice, black pepper, and salt. Mix well and then add the dill and the crayfish tails. Divide the pasta into the serving plates and top it with the crayfish mixture. Garnish with lemon and sprigs. Serve.

Cod with Spinach (Torsk Med Spenat)

Preparation time: 10 minutes
Cook time: 31 minutes
Nutrition facts (per serving): 321 cal (20g fat, 24g protein, g fiber)

This cod with spinach is always a delight on a menu. Now you can make it easily at home by using the following simple ingredients.

Ingredients (2 servings)
1¼ lb. Skrei or white fish
6 oz. mushrooms, sliced
½ onion, sliced
2 tablespoon oil
2 garlic cloves, chopped
9 oz. spinach
3 tablespoon pine nuts
Salt and ground white pepper, to taste

Sauce
¾ cup whipping cream
¾ cup fish stock
4 tablespoon dry white wine
¾ cup grated Parmesan cheese

Preparation
At 425 degrees F, preheat your oven. Slice the fish into four pieces and rub them with black pepper and salt. Add the white wine, stock, and cream to a saucepan and cook for 15 minutes with occasional stirring. Sauté the mushrooms and the onions with oil in a wok until golden. Stir in the garlic and the spinach and cook for 1 minute. Add black pepper and salt, and then spread this mixture in a gratin dish. Place the fish on top and pour the prepared sauce on top. Drizzle Parmesan cheese and pine nuts on top. Bake the fish for 15 minutes in the oven. Serve warm.

Cod with Beans and Bacon (Torsk Med Bönor Och Bacon)

Preparation time: 10 minutes
Cook time: 27 minutes
Nutrition facts (per serving): 378 cal (11g fat, 25g protein, 3g fiber)

If you haven't tried the cod with beans and bacon before, then here comes a simple and easy to cook recipe to share with guests.

Ingredients (2 servings)
¾ lb. French beans, tailed
1 tablespoon olive oil
2 cod steaks
6 slices thin bacon
1 tablespoon pine nuts
6 cherry tomatoes
1 lemon, halved
Salt and black pepper, to taste

Preparation
At 425 degrees F, preheat your oven. Boil the beans in a pan filled with boiling water for 2 minutes, drain, and rinse under cold water. Spread the beans in a baking dish. Toss in black pepper, salt, and olive oil, and then mix well. Place the cod on top and cover it with the bacon rashers. Drizzle olive oil and pine nuts on top. Add the lemon halves and the tomatoes around the cod. Bake the mixture for 20 minutes in the oven. Cover the pan with aluminum foil and bake for almost 5 minutes. Serve warm.

Roasted Haunch of Venison (Rostad Hjortstek)

Preparation time: 10 minutes
Cook time: 32 minutes
Nutrition facts (per serving): 391 cal (7g fat, 27g protein, 2g fiber)

Try cooking the delicious roasted haunch of venison with some unique combination of spices and pasta at home to enjoy the best of the Swedish flavors today!

Ingredients (4 servings)
1 carrot, peeled and sliced
1 celery stick, chopped
1 onion, peeled and sliced
3 bay leaves
5 small sprigs of thyme
8 juniper berries
12 black peppercorns
1 haunch of venison, boned, rolled
Oil for brushing
1 cup beef stock
1 cup red wine
1 tablespoon tomato puree
1 tablespoon red currant jelly

Preparation
At 450 degrees F, preheat your oven. Toss vegetables with the bay leaves, juniper berries, 6 black peppercorns, and thyme in a roasting pan. Place the meat on top of all the veggies and brush it with the boil. Crush the remaining peppercorns and drizzle over the meat. Roast the meat for 20 minutes, then reduce the heat, and roast for 12 minutes. Cover the roasted meat with a foil sheet and leave it

for 20 minutes. Boil the beef stock with tomato puree and wine in a saucepan and then cook until it thickens. Then pour this sauce over the meat. Serve warm.

Frozen Tuber Reindeer (Tjälknöl)

Preparation time: 10 minutes
Cook time: 3 hours
Nutrition facts (per serving): 396 cal (13g fat, 12g protein, 4g fiber)

The reindeer meat is loved by all Swedes, the old and the young, and here's a simple and quick recipe to try the unique flavors at home.

Ingredients (4 servings)
2 lb. frozen boneless piece of reindeer
4 cups of water
1 cup of salt
2 tablespoon sugar
1 bay leaf
1 teaspoon crushed black pepper
2 tablespoon crushed juniper berries

Preparation
Place the reindeer in a roast pan and roast for 2-3 hours until its temperature reaches 150 degrees F. Mix the water with juniper berries, black pepper, bay leaves, sugar, and salt in a saucepan. Boil this mixture, pour this marinade over the meat, and leave it to cool for 5 hours. Remove the prepared meat from the marinade and slice. Serve warm.

Venison with Wild Mushroom Sauce (Hjortsfilé Med Svampsås)

Preparation time: 10 minutes
Cook time: 32 minutes
Nutrition facts (per serving): 492 cal (13g fat, 39g protein, 0.5g fiber)

This venison recipe makes a flavorsome mix of venison with juniper berries and mushroom sauce.

Ingredients (6 servings)
18 oz. venison fillet
1 teaspoon fresh thyme leaves
3 juniper berries, crushed
1 tablespoon olive oil
4 cups fresh wild mushrooms
3 tablespoon butter
2 tablespoon flour
1¼ cups water
½ cup whipping cream
1 mushroom stock cube
1 teaspoon soy sauce
1 tablespoon sherry
Salt and black pepper, to taste

Preparation
Mix the venison with black pepper, salt, oil, crushed juniper berries, and thyme leaves in a plastic bag and marinate for 30 minutes while shaking the bag occasionally. At 400 degrees F, preheat your oven. Sear the venison with oil in a skillet for 5 minutes per side. Spread the venison on a baking sheet and roast for 10-12 minutes in the oven. Cover the meat with foil and leave it for 15 minutes. Sauté the mushrooms with butter in a saucepan for 10 minutes. Stir in flour and mix well.

Add the cream and water and then mix well. Cook for 10 minutes on a simmer. Add salt, black pepper, sherry, and soy sauce. Mix well and serve warm.

Venison with Licorice Sauce (Rådjursfilé Med Lakritssås)

Preparation time: 10 minutes
Cook time: 18 minutes
Nutrition facts (per serving): 457 cal (19g fat, 23g protein, 5g fiber)

Venison with licorice sauce is one delicious way to complete your Swedish menu; here's a recipe that you can try to have a delicious meal.

Ingredients (3 servings)
9 oz. fillet of venison
1 small bunch of thyme
1 tablespoon olive oil
2 tablespoon red wine
2 tablespoon licorice syrup
½ tablespoon butter
1 tablespoon red currant jelly
1 tablespoon apple cider vinegar
Salt and black pepper, to taste

Preparation
Mix the venison with black pepper, salt, oil, and thyme in a Ziploc bag and then seal the bag. Marinate it for 30 minutes. Sear the marinated venison in a greased skillet for 8 minutes. Cover it with a foil sheet and leave it for 20 minutes. Meanwhile, mix the red wine with the licorice syrup in a saucepan. Add the butter and red currant jelly, and then cook until the mixture thickens. Pour this sauce over the meat and serve warm.

Venison with Blackberry Sauce (Hjortfilé Med Björnbärsås)

Preparation time: 10 minutes
Cook time: 12 minutes
Nutrition facts (per serving): 424 cal (16g fat, 19g protein, 14g fiber)

Let's make a spiced chicken liver sauce with these simple ingredients. Mix them together, then cook to have great flavors.

Ingredients (2 servings)
8 black peppercorns
2 juniper berries
2 venison steaks
½ tablespoon olive oil

Sauce
½ tablespoon balsamic vinegar
½ cup beef stock
1 tablespoon red currant jelly
2 oz. blackberries

Preparation
Add the juniper berries and peppercorns to a mortar and crush them using a pestle. Coat the venison steaks with olive oil and rub with the peppercorn mixture. Sear the venison in a pan with oil for 3 minutes per side. Transfer the meat to a plate. Add the balsamic vinegar, redcurrant jelly, and stock to the same pan. Cook for 3 minutes and then puree the mixture. Stir in the blackberries and cook for 3 minutes. Add the venison steak to the sauce. Serve warm.

Reindeer Stew with Mushrooms (Älggryta Med Svamp)

Preparation time: 10 minutes
Cook time: 1 hour 30 minutes
Nutrition facts (per serving): 359 cal (5 g fat, 33g protein, 1g fiber)

Count on this reindeer stew with mushrooms to make your dinner extra special and surprise your loved one with the ultimate Swedish flavors.

Ingredients (4 servings)
2¼ lb. reindeer, diced
2 teaspoon soy sauce
4 tablespoon butter
1 onion, finely chopped
½ leek, sliced
1 ½ teaspoon salt
½ teaspoon ground white pepper
2 cups game beef stock
½ tablespoon balsamic or red wine vinegar
5 juniper berries, crushed
1 teaspoon dried thyme
1 tablespoon blackcurrant jelly
¾ cup cream
3 tablespoon flour
¼ cup of cold water
7 oz. fresh mushrooms
1 tablespoon fresh or frozen lingonberries
6 small sprigs of thyme

Preparation
Soak the reindeer with soy sauce in a bowl. Sear the reindeer in butter in a skillet until brown, and then transfer to a cooking pan. Sauté the onion with butter in

a skillet for 5 minutes, then add leek, and sauté for 3 minutes. Transfer this mixture to the cooking pan. Add the cream, jelly, thyme, juniper berries, vinegar, stock, white pepper, and salt to the cooking pan. Cook for 50 minutes. Whisk the flour with water in a bowl, and pour into the pan, and then cook for 15 minutes until the mixture thickens. Sauté the mushrooms with the butter in a skillet until soft. Add the seasoning and then mix well. Add the mushrooms to the stew and mix well. Garnish with lingonberries and thyme. Serve warm.

Venison burgers (Älgburgare)

Preparation time: 10 minutes
Cook time: 12 minutes
Nutrition facts (per serving): 482 cal (13g fat, 29g protein, 6g fiber)

These venison burgers will melt your heart away with their epic flavors. The burgers are great to serve with cheese and veggies in soft buns.

Ingredients (4 servings)
1 lb. venison, diced or ready ground
3½ oz. smoked pancetta
2 oz. semi-hard Swedish cheese, grated
2 teaspoon sambal Oelek or similar chili paste
1 tablespoon Dijon mustard
2 teaspoon rosemary, chopped
1 unwaxed lemon, zest only
1 teaspoon black pepper, to taste
1 teaspoon oil
1 teaspoon salt
4 brioche burger buns

Preparation
Mix the venison with the pancetta, cheese, Sambal Oelek, mustard, rosemary, lemon zest, black pepper, oil, and salt in a bowl. Coarsely ground this mixture in a food processor. Make four patties from this mixture and sear each patty in a greased skillet for 3 minutes per side. Serve the patties in the burger buns. Enjoy.

Veal Burgers (Wallenbergare)

Preparation time: 15 minutes
Cook time: 20 minutes
Nutrition facts (per serving): 412 cal (9g fat, 13g protein, 0.5g fiber)

The famous veal burgers are here to make your Swedish cuisine extra special. Make them with a mix of veal mince with epice riche for the best taste.

Ingredients (4 servings)
3 slices of white bread, crusts removed
1 lb. veal mince
1 teaspoon salt
1 pinch epice riche
4 egg yolks
1 cup heavy cream
2 tablespoon butter
2 tablespoon oil for frying
Freshly ground white pepper, to taste

Preparation
Grind the bread slices in a food processor and transfer the crumbs to a plate. Mix the veal mince, salt, white pepper, epice riche, egg yolk, and cream in a bowl. Cover and refrigerate the veal mixture for 60 minutes. Make four patties from this mixture. Heat oil and butter for frying in a skillet, coat the patties, with the breadcrumbs, and sear them for 5 minutes per side until golden brown. Serve warm.

Sausage Stroganoff (Korvstroganoff)

Preparation time: 10 minutes
Cook time: 15 minutes
Nutrition facts (per serving): 219 cal (12g fat, 2g protein, 1g fiber)

Best to serve at dinner, this sausage stroganoff can make an energizing meal. Accompany this stroganoff with your favorite boiled pasta.

Ingredients (4 servings)

8 oz. falukorv sausage, diced
1 small onion, sliced
8 oz. can tomato, chopped
½ cup half-fat crème fraiche
1 tablespoon tomato purée
Salt and white pepper to taste

Preparation

Sauté the sausage and onion with oil in a pan for 10 minutes until brown. Stir in the black pepper, salt, tomato puree, crème fraiche, and chopped tomato. Next, mix well. Cook for 5 minutes and then serve warm with rice.

Cold Poached Salmon (Kall Inkokt Lax)

Preparation time: 15 minutes
Cook time: 5 minutes
Nutrition facts (per serving): 456 cal (15g fat, 26g protein, 0.7g fiber)

If you haven't tried the cold poached salmon before, then here comes a simple and easy to cook recipe that you can recreate at home in no time with minimum efforts.

Ingredients (4 servings)

6 cups water
1 small onion, peeled and sliced
1 small Ired onion, peeled and sliced
2 carrots, peeled and sliced
1 unwaxed lemon, sliced
3 dill stalks, leaves removed
3 tablespoon white wine vinegar
1 tablespoon salt
6 white peppercorns
4 whole allspice berries
2 bay leaves
½ teaspoon fennel seeds
1-star anise
4 salmon pieces

Preparation

Add the water, onions, carrots, lemon slices, dill, white wine vinegar, salt, fennel seeds, berries, and all other ingredients, except the salmon, and then cook for 5 minutes. Place the salmon in the marinade and refrigerate it overnight. Remove the fish from the marinade and serve.

Salmon with Cheese
(Lax Med Västerbottensost)

Preparation time: 15 minutes
Cook time: 22 minutes
Nutrition facts (per serving): 319cal (14g fat, 9g protein, 7g fiber)

Salmon with cheese on top is one good option to go for in dinner. Sure, it takes some time to prep, but it's a great taste worth all the time and effort.

Ingredients (6 servings)
7 oz. spinach
1 ¼ lb. salmon fillet, cut into pieces
4 oz. Västerbottensost, Swedish cheese, grated
1 ¼ cups cream
Butter, for greasing
Salt and lemon pepper, to taste

Preparation
At 375 degrees F, preheat your oven. Toss the spinach with lemon pepper and salt in a casserole dish. Place the salmon on top and add cream and grated cheese on top. Bake the salmon for 22 minutes in the oven. Serve warm.

Salmon with Champagne Sauce (Lax Med Champagnesås)

Preparation time: 5 minutes
Cook time: 33 minutes
Nutrition facts (per serving): 376 cal (14g fat, 22g protein, 18g fiber)

This Swedish salmon with champagne sauce recipe will make your day with its delightful taste. Serve warm with your favorite salad.

Ingredients (4 servings)
1 ¼ lb. salmon fillet
1 lb. prawns, peeled and tails removed
6 oz. crayfish tails in brine
1 ¼ cups whipping cream
2 tablespoon lobster stock
2 teaspoon potato flour
½ cup champagne
¼ teaspoon cayenne pepper
Dill, to garnish
Salt and black pepper, to taste

Preparation
At 400 degrees F, preheat your oven. Cut the salmon into four pieces and season them with black pepper and salt in a baking dish. Cook the lobster stock and cream in a pan for 15 minutes. Mix the potato flour with some water in a bowl and pour into the pan. Mix and cook until the sauce thickens. Add the salmon to the sauce and cook for 10 minutes. Stir in the champagne and cayenne pepper. Mix well and add the crayfish and shrimp. Cook for 3 minutes, then garnish with dill. Serve warm.

Salmon Pudding
(Laxpudding)

Preparation time: 15 minutes
Cook time: 65 minutes
Nutrition facts (per serving): 349 cal (7g fat, 29g protein, 3g fiber)

If you want something new flavors in your meals, then this salmon pudding recipe is best to bring variety to the menu.

Ingredients (6 servings)

2 lb. potatoes
1 small onion, sliced
1 tablespoon butter, plus extra for greasing
1 lb. salmon, cut into bite-sized pieces
2 oz. fresh dill finely chopped
3 eggs
1¼ cups milk
½ cup heavy cream
½ teaspoon salt
White pepper to taste

Garnish
4 oz. butter, melted
Dill sprigs
Lemon slices

Preparation
Boil all the potatoes in a saucepan filled with water for 20 minutes, then drain, and peel. Slice and keep the potatoes aside. At 400 degrees F, preheat your oven. Sauté the onion with butter in a pan until soft. Grease a casserole dish and spread half of the potato slices in the dish. Top the potatoes with half of the onions, salmon, and dill, and then repeat the layers. Beat all eggs with white pepper, salt,

cream, and milk in a bowl. Pour this mixture into the salmon layers. Bake the pudding for 45 minutes in the oven and garnish with dill and lemon slices. Serve warm.

Swedish Hash (Pyttipanna)

Preparation time: 15 minutes
Cook time: 15 minutes
Nutrition facts (per serving): 411 cal (12g fat, 8g protein, 7g fiber)

When you can't think of anything to serve in the lunch or dinner, then this Swedish potato hash will help you big time.

Ingredients (5 servings)
1 ½ tablespoon olive oil
5 potatoes, peeled and cubed
1 medium onion, sliced finely
1 cup smoked pork, cubed
½ cup ham, cut into cubed
1 cup sausage, cubed
Salt and black pepper, to taste
Parsley, chopped

Preparation
Add all the hash ingredients to a skillet and sauté until the potatoes are soft. Serve warm.

Salmon Fillets on A Bed of Vegetables (Laxfilé På Grönsaksbädd)

Preparation time: 10 minutes
Cook time: 40 minutes
Nutrition facts (per serving): 326 cal (17g fat, 14g protein, 1.2g fiber)

Here's another classic recipe for your dinner or lunch recipe collection. Serve it with a tangy side salad and enjoy the best of it.

Ingredients (4 servings)
2 salmon fillets
12 oz. new potatoes
1 tablespoon olive oil
7 oz. carrots, peeled and quartered
7 oz. beetroots, peeled and quartered
1 small red onion, peeled and diced
½ red pepper capsicum, julienned
1 teaspoon sea salt
Black pepper, to taste
Dill sprigs

Preparation
At 400 degrees F, preheat your oven. Wash the potatoes and peel them. Dice the potatoes into chunks and pat them dry. Place the potato chunks with oil in a roasting pan. Roast them for 10 minutes. Toss the onion, carrots, beetroots, and red peppers with olive oil in a bowl and spread around the potatoes and roast them for 20 minutes. Rub the salmon with black pepper and salt and place it on top of the veggies. Bake again for 10 minutes. Serve warm.

Salmon in Saffron Sauce (Lax I Saffranssås)

Preparation time: 10 minutes
Cook time: 5 minutes
Nutrition facts (per serving): 367 cal (6g fat, 19g protein, 1.2g fiber)

Try this super tasty salmon in the saffron sauce for your dinner menu, and you'll never stop having it; that's how heavenly the combination tastes.

Ingredients (4 servings)
1 ¼ lb. salmon fillets
7 oz. cherry tomatoes
1 cup half fat creme fraiche
¾ cup water
1 tablespoon tomato purée
½ packet saffron
1 tablespoon corn flour
1 fish stock cube
Salt and black pepper, to taste
2 tablespoon dill, chopped

Preparation
Mix the crème fraiche with water, corn flour, saffron, and tomato puree in a saucepan. Stir in the crumbled fish stock and cook this mixture to a boil. Stir in the tomatoes and the salmon and then cook for 5 minutes. Add black pepper and salt, and then mix well. Garnish with dill. Serve.

Desserts

Poached Pears in Cookie Cups

Preparation time: 10 minutes
Cook time: 20 minutes
Nutrition facts (per serving): 394 cal (16g fat, 3g protein, 6g fiber)

Here's one of the popular and irresistible Swedish dessert that will melt the heart of every sweet tooth. Try it now!

Ingredients (4 servings)
¼ cup butter, cubed
¼ cup sugar
3 tablespoons molasses
⅓ cup ground walnuts
¼ cup all-purpose flour
¼ teaspoon ground ginger

Pears
4 medium Bosc pears
5 cups of water
1 cup of sugar
3 tablespoons grated orange zest
4 teaspoons vanilla extract

Preparation
Mix the molasses with sugar and butter in a saucepan. Boil the mixture and remove it from the heat. Add the ginger, flour and walnuts and then mix well. Divide the batter 3 tablespoons cookies on the baking sheets lined with parchment paper. Bake the cookies for 10 minutes at 350 degrees F until golden brown. Allow the cookies to cool and make a depression in each cookie. Cook the pears with water, vanilla, orange zest, and sugar in a saucepan and cook for 10 minutes. Add the pears to the cookies and serve.

Swedish Christmas Rice Pudding

Preparation time: 15 minutes
Cook time: 60 minutes
Nutrition facts (per serving): 199 cal (7g fat, 6g protein, 0g fiber)

This tomato and cucumber salad is everyone's favorite go-to meal when it comes to serving; you can prepare them in no time without any cooking.

Ingredients (9 servings)
1 cup of water
½ cup uncooked long-grain rice
Dash salt
4 cups of milk
⅔ cup sugar, divided
2 eggs
2 tablespoons butter
1 teaspoon vanilla extract
¼ teaspoon ground cinnamon

Preparation
Boil the water, salt, and rice in a saucepan over medium heat and then cook for 15 minutes on a simmer. Stir in ⅓ cup sugar and milk, and then boil again. Cook for 40 minutes on a simmer. Beat all eggs with the remaining sugar in a bowl. Stir in 2 cups of the hot rice mixture and mix well. Return this hot mixture to the saucepan and cook for 5 minutes on low heat. Stir in the vanilla and butter. Allow the mixture to cool and garnish with cinnamon. Serve.

Viennese Cookies

Preparation time: 15 minutes
Cook time: 15 minutes
Nutrition facts (per serving): 186 cal (11g fat, 2g protein, 1g fiber)

If you haven't tried these Viennese before, then here comes a simple and easy to cook recipe to dazzle at home swiftly.

Ingredients (14 servings)

1 ¼ cups butter, softened
⅔ cup sugar
2 ¼ cups all-purpose flour
1 ⅔ cups ground almonds
1 cup apricot preserves
2 cups semi-sweet chocolate chips
2 tablespoons shortening

Preparation

Beat the softened butter with the sugar in a suitable bowl until fluffy. Stir in the ground almonds and flour and then mix well. Cover and refrigerate it for 1 hour. At 350 degrees F, preheat your oven. Transfer the prepared dough to a floured surface and roll it into ¼ inch thick sheet. Use a 2 ¼ inch cookie cutter to cut cookies out of this sheet. Place the cookies on greased baking sheets. Bake the cookies for 9 minutes until golden brown. Spread the jam on top of half of the cookies. Place the remaining cookies on top. Melt the chocolate chips in a bowl by heating in the microwave. Dip the cookie sandwiches in the chocolate melt and place them on a baking sheet lined with parchment paper. Allow the chocolate to set and then serve.

Cardamom-Blackberry Linzer Cookies

Preparation time: 10 minutes
Cook time: 12 minutes
Nutrition facts (per serving): 188 cal (11g fat, 3g protein, 1g fiber)

The cardamom blackberry cookies are the right fit to serve as a dessert. Here the flour is seasoned with cardamom and the cookies are filled with blackberry jam.

Ingredients (12 servings)

2 cups all-purpose flour
1 cup roasted salted almonds
3 teaspoons ground cardamom
¼ teaspoon salt
1 cup unsalted butter, softened
½ cup 1 teaspoon sugar
1 large egg
1 jar (10 ounces) seedless blackberry jam
1 tablespoon lemon juice
3 tablespoons confectioners' sugar

Preparation

Grind the almonds with ½ cup flour in a food processor. Add the remaining flour, salt and cardamom and then mix well. Beat the butter with ½ cup sugar and the egg in a mixing bowl. Stir in the almonds mixture and then mix until it makes a smooth dough. Divide the prepared dough in half and spread each half into a disc. Cover and refrigerate these discs for 1 hour. At 350 degrees F, preheat your oven. Roll each dough into a ⅛-inch-thick sheet on a floured surface. Cut 1-inch cookies using a cookie cutter and place these cookies on greased baking sheets. Bake the cookies for 12 minutes in the oven until golden brown. Mix the remaining sugar with lemon juice and fruits in a bowl. Spread this mixture over the cookies and garnish with sugar. Serve.

Ginger-Poached Pears

Preparation time: 15 minutes
Cook time: 38 minutes
Nutrition facts (per serving): 429 cal (10g fat, 2g protein, 7g fiber)

If you haven't tried the ginger poached pears before, then here comes a simple and easy to cook recipe that you can easily prepare and cook at home in no time with minimum efforts.

Ingredients (4 servings)

4 medium pears
½ cup ginger ale
½ cup honey
½ cup chopped crystallized ginger
½ cup chopped pecans, toasted

Preparation

At 375 degrees F, preheat your oven. Remove the pear's core, peel, and cut it in half. Place the pears in a 13x9 inch baking. Mix the honey with ginger ale in a saucepan and cook until warm. Pour this mixture over the pears and bake for almost 30 minutes. Transfer the pears to a serving plate. Pour the juices into a saucepan and cook for 8 minutes over medium heat. Pour this mixture over the pears and garnish with pecans. Serve.

Swedish Raspberry Almond Bars

Preparation time: 15 minutes
Cook time: 42 minutes
Nutrition facts (per serving): 165 cal (8g fat, 2g protein, 1g fiber)

The tempting almond bars make a great addition to the dessert menu, and they look amazing when served at the table.

Ingredients (6 servings)
¾ cup butter softened
¾ cup confectioners' sugar
1 ½ cups all-purpose flour
¾ cup seedless raspberry jam
3 large egg whites
6 tablespoons sugar
½ cup sweetened shredded coconut
1 cup sliced almonds, divided
Confectioners' sugar

Preparation
At 350 degrees F, preheat your oven. Beat the softened butter with sugar in a bowl until fluffy. Stir in the flour and mix well. Spread this dough in a 13x9 inch pie pan. Bake it for almost 20 minutes until golden brown. Spread the jam over the crust. Beat the egg whites in a bowl until fluffy. Stir in sugar and continue beating. Fold in ½ cup almonds and coconut and then mix well. Spread this mixture over the jam and layer the remaining almonds on top. Bake the layers for 22 minutes until golden brown. Allow the layers to cool and cut it into bars. Garnish with sugar. Serve.

Chocolate Lace Cookies

Preparation time: 15 minutes
Cook time: 12 minutes
Nutrition facts (per serving): 71 cal (5g fat, 1g protein, 1g fiber)

These chocolate lace cookies will satisfy your sweet tooth in no time. They're very quick to make and bake if you have ready-made dough at home.

Ingredients (14 servings)
½ cup packed brown sugar
⅓ cup butter, cubed
1 tablespoon milk
½ cup ground pecans
3 tablespoons all-purpose flour
1 teaspoon vanilla extract
1 ⅔ cups semisweet chocolate chips

Preparation
At 350 degrees F, preheat your oven. Mix the milk with brown sugar, milk, and butter in a saucepan. Mix and cook this mixture for almost 4 minutes until it thickens. Add the vanilla, flour, and pecans, then mix well. Drop ½ teaspoon of the batter onto the baking sheets lined with parchment paper and add the remaining batter in the same manner. Bake the cookies for 7 minutes until golden. Allow the cookies to cool. Melt the chocolate in a bowl by heating it in the microwave. Add 1 teaspoon of chocolate on top of each cookie. Allow the cookies to cool. Serve.

Swedish Cream Apple Rings

Preparation time: 15 minutes
Cook time: 30 minutes
Nutrition facts (per serving): 290 cal (12g fat, 4g protein, 1g fiber)

Swedish cream apple rings are another Swedish-inspired delight that you should definitely try on this cuisine. Serve with chocolate syrup.

Ingredients (10 servings)
1 package active dry yeast
¼ cup warm water
4 cups all-purpose flour
¼ cup sugar
½ teaspoon salt
¾ cup cold butter, cubed
1 cup heavy whipping cream
¼ cup evaporated milk
3 large egg yolks

Filling
2 cups apples, chopped
½ cup raisins
¼ cup cinnamon-sugar

Glaze
2 cups confectioners' sugar
1 teaspoon vanilla extract
3 tablespoons milk

Preparation
Mix the yeast with hot water in a small bowl. Stir in the salt, sugar, and flour, and then mix well. Cut in butter and mix until crumbly. Stir in the yeast

mixture, egg yolks, milk, and cream and then mix until it makes a smooth dough. Cover the dough and refrigerate it overnight. Mix apples with cinnamon sugar and raisins in a bowl. Spread each half of the dough in a 13x7 inch rectangle and add half of the filling on top. Roll the dough, bring both the edges together to make a ring, and pinch the edges to make a complete ring. Place both the rings in a baking sheet with their seam side down. Cover and leave the rings for 45 minutes. At 375 degrees F, preheat your oven. Bake the rings for 30 minutes and then allow them to cool. Mix the sugar with vanilla and milk in a bowl. Pour this glaze over the rings. Allow the rings to cool and serve.

Cinnamon Rolls

Preparation time: 10 minutes
Cook time: 25 minutes
Nutrition facts (per serving): 199 cal (8g fat, 2g protein, 1g fiber)

What about delicious cinnamon rolls? If you haven't tried them before, now is the time to cook these fabulous rolls at home using simple and healthy ingredients.

Ingredients (12 servings)
1 package active dry yeast
1 tablespoon sugar
¼ cup warm water
1 cup milk
⅓ cup instant vanilla pudding mix
1 large egg
¼ cup butter, melted
1 teaspoon salt
3 ½ cups all-purpose flour

Filling
¾ cup sugar
1 tablespoon ground cinnamon
¼ cup butter, melted

Frosting
½ cup butter softened
2 teaspoons vanilla extract
1 teaspoon water
1 ¾ cups confectioners' sugar

Preparation

Mix the yeast with 1 tablespoon sugar and warm water in a bowl and leave it for 5 minutes. Beat the pudding mix with milk in a bowl on low speed for 1 minute. Beat in the melted butter, yeast mixture, salt, 2 cups flour, and egg and, then mix well until smooth. Add the remaining flour and mix until it makes smooth dough. Transfer the prepared dough to a floured surface and knead for 8 minutes. Place the dough in a greased bowl, cover it with a plastic sheet and leave it for 1 hour.

Mix the cinnamon with the sugar. Divide the dough in half. Roll each half of the dough into an 18x10 inch rectangle on a floured surface and brush its top with half of the butter. Drizzle half of the cinnamon mixture on top and then roll it and pinch the edges. Slice the roll into 12 slices and place these slices on a 13x9 inch baking sheet. Cover and leave them for 45 minutes. Bake the cinnamon rolls at 350 degrees F for 25 minutes until golden brown. Allow them to cool. Beat the vanilla with sugar and water in a bowl and pour over the cinnamon rolls. Serve.

Apple and Almond Tart

Preparation time: 10 minutes
Cook time: 48 minutes
Nutrition facts (per serving): 379 cal (11g fat, 34g protein, 3g fiber)

If you haven't tried the apple and almond tart before, then here comes a simple and easy to cook recipe for a yummy dessert!

Ingredients (8 servings)
Pastry
1¼ cups all-purpose flour
3 tablespoon caster sugar
½ cup butter, cut into cubes
1 egg yolk

Filling
⅓ cup butter softened
⅝ cup ground almonds
7 tablespoon caster sugar
1 large egg
1 unwaxed lemon, zest, and juice
2 red-skinned apples

Topping
3 tablespoon butter
1 tablespoon flour
3 tablespoon caster sugar
2 tablespoon liquid glucose
½ cup flaked almonds

Preparation

Mix the flour with sugar and butter in a food processor for 15 seconds. Then add the egg yolk and blend for 30 seconds. Spread this mixture in a tart pan and Bake for almost 12 minutes. Mix the sugar, egg, lemon zest, and ground almonds in a large bowl. Toss in the apples and lemon juice, and then mix well. Spread this mixture into the crust. Bake the tart for 25 minutes in the oven. Prepare the topping by mixing its ingredients. Spread this mixture on top of the filling. Bake again for 10 minutes. Slice and serve.

Spiced Apple Compote
(Kryddig Äppelkompott)

Preparation time: 15 minutes
Cook time: 20 minutes
Nutrition facts (per serving): 347 cal (5g fat, 7g protein, 5g fiber)

A dessert that has no parallel: the Swedish apple compote is made with a mix of apples and orange juice.

Ingredients (12 servings)
3 large apples, cored and diced
½ vanilla pod, split
3 ½ tablespoon caster sugar
3 ½ tablespoon soft brown sugar
1 short cinnamon stick
2-star anise
2 tablespoon orange juice

Instructions
Add the apples, vanilla, sugars, cinnamon, star anise, and orange juice to a saucepan. Cook this mixture for almost 20 minutes with occasional stirring. Allow this mixture to cool and then discard the cinnamon and star anise. Mash well and serve.

Bilberry Crumble (Blåbärssmulpaj)

Preparation time: 15 minutes
Cook time: 45 minutes
Nutrition facts (per serving): 221 cal (3 g fat, 4 g protein, 2.8g fiber)

Yes, you can make something as delicious as this bilberry crumble by using only basic dessert and cookies ingredients and some simple techniques.

Ingredients (8 servings)
Pastry
8 oz. all-purpose flour
4 ½ oz. cold butter, cubed
1 oz. icing sugar
1 egg, beaten
2 tablespoon water

Filling
1 lb. bilberries, fresh or frozen
4 ½ oz. caster sugar
4 tablespoon potato flour

Crumble topping
5 oz. all-purpose flour
2 ½ oz. caster sugar
1 tablespoon vanilla sugar
4 oz. salted butter

Preparation
Mix the flour with sugar and butter in a food processor for 15 seconds. Then add the egg and water and blend for 30 seconds. Spread this dough in a 9-inch tart pan. Mix the sugar, potato flour, and berries in a bowl. Spread the berries in

the crust. Prepare the topping by mixing its ingredients. Spread this mixture on top of the filling. Bake again for 45 minutes. Slice and serve.

Beetroot Ice Cream (Rödbetsglass)

Preparation time: 15 minutes
Cook time: 5 minutes
Nutrition facts (per serving): 357 cal (12g fat, 5.5g protein, 1.4g fiber)

Try this beetroot ice cream on your Swedish menu. The sweet combination of beetroots with cream and milk is bliss for all the sweet tooth fans!

Ingredients (6 servings)
10 oz. beetroot, peeled and diced
1 oz. fresh ginger, peeled and grated
½ tablespoon lemon juice
1 tablespoon cold water
3 oz. whole milk
1 cup heavy cream
1 teaspoon vanilla paste
1 egg
6 tablespoon granulated cane sugar

Preparation
Puree the beetroot with 1 tablespoon water, ginger, and lemon juice in a blender for 5 minutes until smooth. Strain this mixture through a cheesecloth. Mix the milk with the vanilla paste and cream in a saucepan, warm it for 5 minutes, and then remove it from the heat. Beat the egg in a bowl for 2 minutes until fluffy. Add the sugar and blend well. Stir in the beetroot mixture and mix well. Add this ice cream mixture to the ice cream machine and churn until set. Freeze the ice cream for 4 hours. Scoop out the ice cream. Serve.

Blackberry Tart

Preparation time: 15 minutes
Cook time: 20 minutes
Nutrition facts (per serving): 169 cal (12g fat, 8g protein, 4g fiber)

The famous Swedish blackberry tart is essential to try on the Swedish dessert menu. Savor cooking it at home with these healthy ingredients and enjoy it.

Ingredients (6 servings)
Pastry
¾ cup butter
1 ¼ cups all-purpose flour
7 tablespoon caster sugar
½ teaspoon baking powder
1 pinch of salt

Filling
⅓ cup almond flour
1 lb. blackberries
6 ½ tablespoon caster sugar
1 tablespoon potato flour

Glaze
3 tablespoon blackberry jelly

Preparation
Mix the flour with sugar, baking powder, salt, and butter in a food processor for 15 seconds. Spread this mixture in a 9-inch tart pan and almonds on top of the crust. Mix the blackberries with the potato flour and sugar in a bowl. Add this mixture on top of the almond. Bake the tart for 20 minutes in the oven. Garnish the pie with the jelly and serve

Chocolate Balls (Chokladbollar)

Preparation time: 10 minutes
Nutrition facts (per serving): 408 cal (20g fat, 34g protein, 0.4g fiber)

If you want something exotic on your dessert menu, then nothing can taste better than these delicious chocolate balls.

Ingredients (6 servings)

½ cup caster sugar
3 ½ oz. unsalted butter
1 teaspoon vanilla extract
3 tablespoon strong coffee, hot
3 tablespoon cocoa powder
1 pinch sea salt
1 ½ cups rolled oats
1 ¾ oz. desiccated coconut

Preparation

Beat the butter with vanilla and sugar in a bowl until fluffy. Mix cocoa powder with coffee in a bowl. Stir in the butter mixture and mix well. Add the oats and the salt and then mix well. Make small balls from this mixture and roll them in coconut. Serve.

Chocolate Fondants (Chokladfondant)

Preparation time: 10 minutes
Cook time: 13 minutes
Nutrition facts (per serving): 202 cal (7g fat, 6g protein, 1.3g fiber)

If you're a chocolate lover, then this Swedish dessert recipe is the right fit for you. Try this at home and cook in no time.

Ingredients (6 servings)
2 teaspoon cocoa powder
7 tablespoon unsalted butter
5 ¼ oz. dark chocolate
2 eggs
2 egg yolks
3 tablespoon dark muscovado sugar
1 tablespoon vanilla sugar
½ teaspoon ground ginger
6 tablespoon cranberries
3 tablespoon caster sugar
2 tablespoon water
¾ cup cream, whipped
Icing sugar, for dusting
Butter for greasing

Preparation
At 400 degrees F, preheat your oven. Grease six ramekins with butter and dust them with cocoa powder. Melt the chocolate and butter in a saucepan over medium heat. Beat all eggs with sugars and yolks in a bowl until fluffy. Stir in the melted chocolate and then mix well. Divide the mixture in the ramekins, bake for almost 8 minutes, and then allow them to cool. Mix the water, cranberries, and sugar in a saucepan. Cook this mixture for almost 5 minutes, and then allow it to cool. Garnish the fondants with sugar, cream, and berries. Serve.

Chocolate Truffles (Chokladtryfflar)

Preparation time: 10 minutes
Cook time: 5 minutes
Nutrition facts (per serving): 493 cal (18g g fat, 9g protein, 3g fiber)

The famous Swedish truffles are another special dessert to try on the Swedish menu. Enjoy making them at home with these healthy ingredients.

Ingredients (8 servings)

7 oz. dark chocolate, 70% cocoa
3 tablespoon butter, cut into small cubes
4 tablespoon crystallized candied ginger
1 orange, zest
¾ cup heavy cream
⅓ cup light muscovado sugar
1 pinch sea salt
10 oz. milk chocolate, cut into squares
2 tablespoon cocoa powder, sifted

Preparation

Add the chocolate and butter to a bowl and melt by heating in the microwave. Mix the ginger with orange zest in a bowl. Mix the cream with sugar in a saucepan and cook for 1 minute with occasional stirring. Stir in the chocolate melt and salt, and then mix well. Add the ginger orange mix, and then mix well. Cover and refrigerate this mixture for 1 hour. Make small balls from this mixture. Refrigerate the truffles for 30 minutes. Melt the remaining chocolate in a bowl. Dip the truffles in the chocolate and coat them with the cocoa powder. Serve.

Cinnamon Ice Cream (Kanelglass)

Preparation time: 15 minutes
Cook time: 15 minutes
Nutrition facts (per serving): 201cal (6g fat, 4g protein, 0.6g fiber)

This cinnamon ice cream has no parallel; it has a strong cinnamon flavor and creamy texture. Try it with cinnamon and nuts toppings for the best taste.

Ingredients (4 servings)
1 cup milk
1 cinnamon stick
3 egg yolks
½ cup of sugar
1 teaspoon vanilla sugar
1 tablespoon ground cinnamon
2 cups whipping cream

Preparation
Add the milk and cinnamon stick to a saucepan and cook this mixture to boil. Then remove it from the heat. Beat the egg yolks with the sugars in a bowl and then stir in the cinnamon. Remove the cinnamon stick from the milk and pour this milk into the egg yolks mixture. Mix well and return this mixture to a saucepan. Next, cook for 10 minutes on low heat. Stir in the cream and mix well. Allow the custard to cool and cover with a cling film. Refrigerate the custard for 1 hour. Serve.

Plum Trifle (Plommontrifli)

Preparation time: 10 minutes
Cook time: 5 minutes
Nutrition facts (per serving): 203 cal (7g fat, 3g protein, 1g fiber)

The Swedish plum trifle is great to serve with all the hot beverages, and it's super popular for the sweet and earthy taste.

Ingredients (8 servings)
1 lb. plums, pitted, and chopped
2 tablespoon water
3 ½ oz. caster sugar
2 teaspoon vanilla sugar
2 tablespoon Madeira
4 ½ oz. Amaretti biscuits
1 cup whipping cream
1 teaspoon almond essence
1 tablespoon flaked almonds

Preparation
Boil the sugars with water and Madeira in a saucepan and cook until dissolved. Stir in the plums and cook for 5 minutes. Allow the mixture to cool. Layer the serving bowls with half of the biscuits. Add half of the plum's mixture into the bowls. Add a layer of cream and then repeat the layers of the garnish with almonds. Serve.

Red Currant Sorbet (Rödvinbärssorbet)

Preparation time: 10 minutes
Nutrition facts (per serving): 58 cal (1.4g fat, 1g protein, 2g fiber)

This sorbet is worth the try as it tastes so unique and exotic. This dessert is definitely a must on the Swedish menu.

Ingredients (6 servings)
5 cups redcurrants
1 ¾ cups caster sugar
1 medium orange, zest, and juice
4 tablespoon orange liqueur

Preparation
Cook the red currants with sugar, orange zest, juice, and orange liqueur in a saucepan. Mix well until sugar is dissolved. Freeze this mixture in a container and then blend this frozen syrup until crushed. Serve.

Rhubarb and Strawberry Jam

Preparation time: 15 minutes
Cook time: 5 minutes
Nutrition facts (per serving): 289 cal (13g fat, 3g protein, 2g fiber)

If you haven't tried the rhubarb and strawberry jam before, then here comes a simple and easy to cook recipe to serve at home swiftly and effortlessly!

Ingredients (16 servings)
4 cups rhubarb
4 cups strawberries, hulled and halved
3 ⅓ cups jam sugar
1 teaspoon vanilla powder
1 teaspoon butter

Preparation
Mix the strawberries with jam sugar and vanilla powder in a saucepan. Next, cook until the sugar is melted. Stir in the rhubarb and boil this mixture for 5 minutes. Remove the prepared mixture from the heat. Stir in the butter and then allow the jam to cool. Mash this mixture until smooth and then divide this jam in sterilized jars and cover. Serve.

Rye pancakes (Rågpannkakor)

Preparation time: 15 minutes
Cook time: 10 minutes
Nutrition facts (per serving): 650 cal (36g fat, 12g protein, 0g fiber)

The famous rye pancakes are essential on the Swedish dessert menu. Try baking at home with these healthy ingredients and enjoy them.

Ingredients (4 servings)
¾ cup dark rye flour
¾ cup white rye flour
1 ½ teaspoon baking powder
¼ teaspoon salt
¾ cup milk, skimmed
2 tablespoon *ljus sirap* or any other sugar syrup
4 medium eggs, separated
Oil for spraying

Preparation
Mix the flours with baking powder, salt, milk, ijus, and egg yolks in a bowl until smooth. Beat the egg whites in a mixer until fluffy and add this foam to the batter. Mix gently and keep it aside. Grease a skillet and set it over medium heat. Add ¼ of the batter and cook for 45 seconds per side. Serve.

Saffron and White Chocolate Truffles

Preparation time: 15 minutes
Cook time: 4 minutes
Nutrition facts (per serving): 228 cal (6g fat, 4g protein, 3g fiber)

These white chocolate truffles are one good option to go for in the desserts. You can also keep them ready and stored and then use them instead as instant desserts.

Ingredients (8 servings)
7 oz. white chocolate
7 tablespoon whipping cream
2 teaspoon honey
1 tablespoon butter
1 small packet of saffron threads
½ cup icing sugar

Preparation
Melt the chocolate in a bowl by heating it in the microwave. Mix the cream, saffron, honey, and butter in a saucepan and then boil the mixture. Pour this mixture into the melted chocolate, and then mix well for 3 minutes. Cover and refrigerate the mixture for 30 minutes. Make small balls from this mixture and roll them in the sugar to coat. Serve.

Swedish Nuts

Preparation time: 10 minutes
Cook time: 30 minutes
Nutrition facts (per serving): 298 cal (26g fat, 3.1g protein, 1g fiber)

If you haven't tried the crispy and coated pecans before, then here comes a simple and easy to cook recipe to recreate at home in no time with minimum efforts.

Ingredients (16 servings)

2 egg whites
1 cup white sugar
1 pinch salt
½ teaspoon vanilla extract
1-pound pecan halves
½ cup butter

Preparation

Beat the egg whites with sugar in a bowl until fluffy. Stir the salt, vanilla extract, and butter, and then mix well. Fold in the pecans and mix to coat well. Spread this pecan mixture on a baking sheet and bake for 30 minutes. Allow them to cool and serve.

Saffron Puddings with Raspberry Jam

Preparation time: 10 minutes
Cook time: 40 minutes
Nutrition facts (per serving): 186 cal (12g fat, 4g protein, 2.5g fiber)

Without this saffron pudding, it seems like the Swedish dessert menu is incomplete. Try it with different variations of toppings.

Ingredients (8 servings)
3 green cardamom pods
1 sachet saffron threads
½ tablespoon vanilla sugar
2 eggs
1¼ cup of rice pudding (risgrynsgröt)
4 tablespoon almonds, chopped
½ cup milk
¾ cup whipping cream
Butter for greasing

Preparation
At 350 degrees F, preheat your oven. Grease 6 ramekins with butter. Crush the cardamom seeds in a mortar with a pestle. Add the vanilla sugar and saffron and mix well. Beat all eggs in a bowl and then stir in rice pudding, saffron mixture, cream, milk, and almonds. Mix well and then divide this mixture in the ramekins. Bake for almost 40 minutes. Serve.

Strawberry Compote (Jordgubbskompott)

Preparation time: 10 minutes
Cook time: 10 minutes
Nutrition facts (per serving): 241 cal (4g fat, 2g protein, 1.1g fiber)

Here comes a dessert that's cherished by all. The strawberry isn't only served as a dessert, but it's also a good spread for your breakfast bread.

Ingredients (12 servings)
2 ¼ lb. strawberries
1 lemon, juice only
2 ¼ lb. jam sugar
1 teaspoon butter

Preparation
Mix the strawberries with lemon juice, sugar, and butter in a saucepan and cook for 3 minutes with occasional stirring until the sugar is dissolved. Mash this strawberry mixture and remove the scum from the compote. Finally, allow the compote to cool for 15 minutes. Divide the compote into the glasses and serve.

Semla

Preparation time: 10 minutes
Cook time: 10 minutes
Nutrition facts (per serving): 176 cal (17g fat, 7g protein, 3g fiber)

It's truly if the Swedish menu is incomplete without a Semla. These are soft and fluffy buns stuffed with marzipan filling.

Ingredients (6 servings)
Buns
3 ½ oz. butter
2 ¼ cup milk
1 ⅔ oz. fresh yeast
1 teaspoon crushed cardamom
½ teaspoon salt
2 oz. sugar
19 oz. plain flour
1 beaten egg for brushing

Filling
1 cup marzipan, grated
½ cup milk
2 ¼ cup whipping cream
Decoration
Icing sugar for dusting

Preparation
Mix the milk with butter in a pan at 110 degrees F and then remove from the heat. Stir in the yeast and cardamom. Next, mix well. Add the sugar, salt, and flour, then mix until it makes smooth dough. Cover and leave the dough for 40 minutes. Divide the dough into buns and place them on a baking sheet. Bake for almost 10 minutes at 400 degrees F in the oven. Allow the buns to cool. Mix the

grated marzipan with milk and cream in a bowl. Make a hole in the buns and stuff them with the marzipan filling. Garnish the buns with icing sugar. Serve.

Drinks

Cranberry Glogg

Preparation time: 10 minutes
Cook time: 15 minutes
Nutrition facts (per serving): 268 cal (0g fat, 1g protein, 1g fiber)

The cranberry glogg is the most popular traditional Swedish drink to try for every occasion and special celebration. It has a sweet and strong mix of flavors that you'll love.

Ingredients (7 servings)
4 cups cranberry juice
2 cups ruby port wine
1 cup golden raisins
¼ cup sugar
2 cinnamon sticks
4 cardamom pods, crushed
6 whole cloves
Cinnamon sticks

Preparation
Add sugar, raisins, wine, and cranberry juice in a large saucepan. Add cloves, cinnamon, and cardamom to a cheesecloth and tie the spices. Place the spice bag in the saucepan. Cook this mixture on a simmer for 15 minutes. Discard the spice bag and pour the glogg into serving glasses.

Strawberry Smoothie (Jordgubbssmoothie)

Preparation time: 5 minutes
Nutrition facts (per serving): 112 cal (2g fat, 4 protein, 3g fiber)

Beat the heat and try the famous strawberry smoothie with a mix of strawberries and bananas. The combination is super refreshing and healthy.

Ingredients (1 serving)

8 oz. strawberries
1 small banana, peeled
5 tablespoon orange juice
1 ¾ cups low-fat yogurt
Honey or sugar
Ice cubes

Preparation

Blend the strawberries with banana, orange juice, yogurt, and honey in a blender. Serve with ice cubes. Enjoy.

Warm Sambucus

Preparation time: 5 minutes
Cook time: 5 minutes
Nutrition facts (per serving): 103cal (7g fat, 3g protein, 1g fiber)

The Swedish Sambucus is loved by all due to its refreshing elderflower flavors.
Serve it warm for the best taste and flavor.

Ingredients (4 servings)
1 ¼ cups elderflower cordial syrup
10 juniper berries
½ vanilla pod, bean
1 bottle dry white wine
5 tablespoon Absolut vodka

Preparation
Add the elderflower syrup and juniper berries to a saucepan and boil. Remove
the pan from the heat, add vanilla seeds, and then leave the mixture for 2 hours.
Strain the mixture through a sieve. Add vodka and wine. Mix well and serve.

Rhubarb cocktails (Rabarberdrinkar)

Preparation time: 10 minutes
Cook time: 15 minutes
Nutrition facts (per serving): 117 cal (14g fat, 12g protein, 0g fiber)

The Swedish rhubarb cocktail is great to serve on all special occasions and dinner. It has this appealing mix of gingery flavors.

Ingredients (10 servings)
7 cups rhubarb, chopped
1 oz. ginger, chopped
2 oz. crystallized ginger, chopped
1 ½ cups sugar

Preparation
Add rhubarb to a saucepan, insert ginger, and then sugar to the pan. Pour in enough water to cover the rhubarb. Cook the mixture for 10 minutes on a simmer. Strain the mixture through a fine sieve and allow the juice to cool. Serve.

Redcurrant Smoothie
(Röda Vinbärssmoothie)

Preparation time: 10 minutes
Nutrition facts (per serving): 142 cal (3g fat, 6.3g protein, 1g fiber)

Serve this super delicious of redcurrants with banana and cranberries. Use honey to add a mildly sweet flavor to this creamy combination.

Ingredients (8 servings)
8 oz. red currants, fresh or frozen
1 small banana, peeled
5 tablespoons of cranberries
1 cup low-fat yogurt
Honey or sugar
Ice cubes

Preparation
Blend the red currants with yogurt, cordial, and a banana in a blender until smooth. Add honey and ice cubes, mix well, and serve.

Redcurrant Cordial (Vinbärssaft)

Preparation time: 5 minutes
Cook time: 15 minutes
Nutrition facts (per serving): 156 cal (0g fat, 0.7g protein, 1.4g fiber)

This redcurrant cordial drink is all that you need to celebrate the holidays. Keep the drink ready in your refrigerator for quick serving.

Ingredients (8 serving)

1 lb. red currants
6 oz. caster sugar

Preparation

Add ½ cup water, red currants, and sugar to a saucepan. Cook this mixture to a boil and cook for 10 minutes. Strain this mixture through the cheesecloth. Allow the drink to cool and serve.

Raspberry Cordial (Hallonsaft)

Preparation time: 5 minutes
Cook time: 15 minutes
Nutrition facts (per serving): 131 cal (11g fat, 10g protein, 0.3g fiber)

The raspberry cordial is another classic way to enjoy the tempting mix of a raspberry extract with sugar and citric acid.

Ingredients (6 servings)
6 cups raspberries
4 cups of water
2 ½ cups granulated sugar
2 tablespoon citric acid crystals

Preparation
Boil the berries with citric acid, sugar, and water in a large saucepan and cook for 10 minutes on a simmer. Remove the prepared mixture from the heat and allow it to cool. Strain this mixture through a cheesecloth. Allow the drink to cool and serve.

Polar Bear Cocktail (Isbjörn Eller Blue Lagoon)

Preparation time: 5 minutes
Nutrition facts (per serving): 110 cal (0g fat, 0g protein, 1g fiber)

Try this special Swedish vodka drink with a refreshing hint of lemonade. It's so great for special dinners and festive celebrations.

Ingredients (4 servings)
Ice cubes
2 oz. vodka
1 oz. blue curacao
6 oz. lemonade

Preparation
Add ice cubes to a highball glass. Pour in vodka, blue curacao, and lemonade. Serve.

Elderflower Cordial Drink
(Fläderblomssaft)

Preparation time: 5 minutes
Cook time: 10 minutes
Nutrition facts (per serving): 122 cal (13g fat, 12g protein, 2.3g fiber)

Here's a special elderflower cordial syrup drink, which is great to serve at special dinners and memorable celebrations.

Ingredients (16 servings)
40 large elderflower heads
3 lemons
8 cups of water
8 cups granulated sugar
4 tablespoon citric acid

Preparation
Boil 8 cups of water with sugar in a saucepan. Mix well, add citric acid, lemon juice, and then the elderflower. Then remove it from the heat. Pour this mixture into a mason jar, add the lid, and then leave it for 5 days. Strain the mixture through a cheesecloth. Enjoy.

Sloe Snaps

Preparation time: 5 minutes
Nutrition facts (per serving): 114 cal (1g fat, 2g protein, 1g fiber)

With its deep red color and fruity flavor, the sloe snap makes a great aperitif to serve. Garnish the drink with your favorite toppings.

Ingredients (6 servings)
2 cups ripe sloes
½ cup of sugar
1 bottle vodka

Preparation
Mix all the ingredients in a mason and cover with its lid. Place this jar in a dark place for 4 weeks, strain, and serve.

If you liked Swedish recipes, discover to how cook DELICIOUS recipes from **Balkan** countries!

Within these pages, you'll learn 35 authentic recipes from a Balkan cook. These aren't ordinary recipes you'd find on the Internet, but recipes that were closely guarded by our Balkan mothers and passed down from generation to generation.

Main Dishes, Appetizers, and Desserts included!

If you want to learn how to make Croatian green peas stew, and 32 other authentic Balkan recipes, then start with our book!

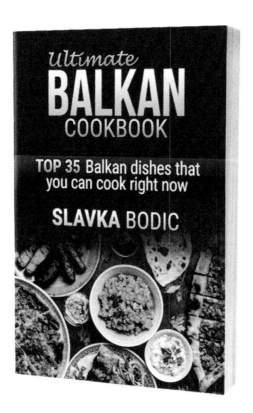

Order at www.balkanfood.org/cook-books/ for only $2,99

If you're a **Mediterranean** dieter who wants to know the secrets of the Mediterranean diet, dieting, and cooking, then you're about to discover how to master cooking meals on a Mediterranean diet right now!

In fact, if you want to know how to make Mediterranean food, then this new e-book - "The 30-minute Mediterranean diet" - gives you the answers to many important questions and challenges every Mediterranean dieter faces, including:

- How can I succeed with a Mediterranean diet?
- What kind of recipes can I make?
- What are the key principles to this type of diet?
- What are the suggested weekly menus for this diet?
- Are there any cheat items I can make?

... and more!

If you're serious about cooking meals on a Mediterranean diet and you really want to know how to make Mediterranean food, then you need to grab a copy of "The 30-minute Mediterranean diet" right now.
Prepare **111 recipes with several ingredients in less than 30 minutes**!

Order at www.balkanfood.org/cook-books/ for only $2,99

What could be better than a home-cooked meal? Maybe only a **Greek** homemade meal.

Do not get discouraged if you have no Greek roots or friends. Now you can make a Greek food feast in your kitchen.

This ultimate Greek cookbook offers you 111 best dishes of this cuisine! From more famous gyros to more exotic *Kota Kapama* this cookbook keeps it easy and affordable.

All the ingredients necessary are wholesome and widely accessible.
The author's picks are as flavorful as they are healthy. The dishes described in this cookbook are "what Greek mothers have made for decades."

Full of well-balanced and nutritious meals, this handy cookbook includes many vegan options. Discover a plethora of benefits of Mediterranean cuisine, and you may fall in love with cooking at home.

Inspired by a real food lover, this collection of delicious recipes will taste buds utterly satisfied.

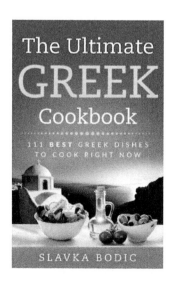

Order at www.balkanfood.org/cook-books/ for only $2,99

Maybe to try exotic **Syrian** cuisine?

From succulent *sarma*, soups, warm and cold salads to delectable desserts, the plethora of flavors will satisfy the most jaded foodie. Have a taste of a new culture with this **traditional Syrian cookbook**.

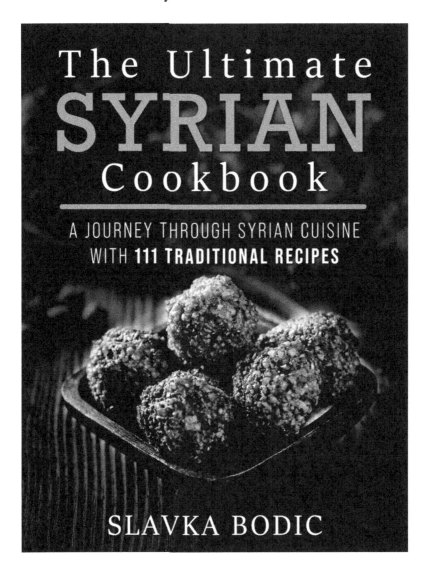

Order at www.balkanfood.org/cook-books/ for only $2,99

Maybe **Polish** cuisine?

Order at www.balkanfood.org/cook-books/ for only $2,99

Or **Peruvian**?

Order at www.balkanfood.org/cook-books/ for only $2,99

ONE LAST THING

If you enjoyed this book or found it useful, I'd be very grateful if you could find the time to post a short review on Amazon. Your support really does make a difference and I read all the reviews personally, so I can get your feedback and make this book even better.

Thanks again for your support!

Please send me your feedback at

www.balkanfood.org

Printed in Great Britain
by Amazon

39978086R00091